All the Happy Families

All the Happy Families

Exploring the Varieties of Family Life

Paul Bohannan

McGraw-Hill Book Company

New York   St. Louis   San Francisco   Hamburg   Mexico   Toronto

1 2 3 4 5 6 7 8 9 D O C D O C 8 7 6 5

ISBN 0-07-006432-6

LIBRARY OF CONGRESS CATALOGING IN PUBLICATION DATA

Bohannan, Paul.
All the happy families.
Bibliography: p.
1. Family—United States.   2. Divorce—United States.
I. Title.
HQ536.B62   1985   306.8′5′0973   84-11232
ISBN 0-07-006432-6

Book design by Barbara Marks

Contents

Introduction:
Taking a New Look
at Families

The family is the most adaptable of all human institutions, changing with every social demand. The family does not break in a storm as oak or pine trees do, but bends before the wind like the bamboo tree in Oriental tales, and springs up again. Its suppleness makes the family tough enough to resist any threat to its well-being.

At this instant in history, storms blown by all kinds of vested interests are buffeting the family as never before. Doctrines about what the family is—mixed from equal parts of myth and delusion about what it has been and hopes about what it might become—are loudly pronounced against a background of rampant sentimentality about what it ought to be.

The storm engulfing the family right now is of immense evolutionary importance. For the first time in history, culture has become refined enough to give us the opportunity to take a really new developmental step. We can overcome some of the limitations that constrain us because we are mammals (as are hedgehogs and foxes and chimpanzees). We are today in a position totally to recast the roles of the family and how we play them; no earlier generation had that opportunity. Some historical eras had "good" families (the definition changes), while in other eras many people refused to participate in the family. But the choice in the past was different: it was

1

up to an individual to opt into the family or opt out of it. Men who opted out of it gave up the opportunity for legitimate (that is, socially recognized) paternity, but otherwise their social range was little affected. Women who opted out of the family were more disadvantaged: most of them gave up not only maternity, but love and sexual intimacy. They could take part only within limits in the culture of the outside world.

Today we can have it both ways—we can opt into the family without becoming its prisoners (women its central prisoners, men the guards, but as irrevocably sentenced). The defenses of those who fear this change take the form that Erich Fromm fifty years ago called "escape from freedom."

The power of technology (including safe and easy contraception) has made it possible in our century for women to live full sex lives without having to be tied to childbearing. They are able to turn far more of their energies to other pursuits. Culture is not merely changing, it is also changing the limitations placed on us by our animality. This has happened before: as the Industrial Age dawned, the steam engine changed the physical limitations and put women "into the home" by the simple device of taking men out of it. But we do not remember the agony of the family at that time. Today instead of an industrial we are facing a biological revolution. *That* is what we are afraid of!

Whether we like it or not, the change in the position of women (and hence of men) that has been made possible by modern science has created a vast change in the family. Some people—more men than women, but some women too—feel discommoded by the change. In their discomfort, they invoke the "sacredness" of the family to try to turn back the future. If you look at it squarely, the family is just another social institution, no more sacred than the church or the government or the corporation. The idea of its "sacred" importance arises primarily because the family is the back-up institution for everything—and nothing much today backs up the family. Most of us know more about families than we do about churches or governments or corporations for the simple reason that almost all of us grew up in a family, which makes everybody an expert.

But today our ideas about families are out of phase with the families we actually live in. Some people, terrified, react by glorifying the past. We seldom compare the family of the "good old days" with the considerable virtues of families now. Rather, when we memorialize the virtues of "traditional" families, it is usually for the purpose of showing up what we imagine to be the flaws in the family of our own time—callous selfishness and social disruption. Many of our truisms about traditional families are in fact historically false, backed up only by personal memories (real or imagined) of Grandma or good old Uncle Ralph. But, truly, families in the old days were *not* demonstrably closer or more efficient; historians find just as many horror stories and as many good families then as now.

"Family" is a code word for our deeper views of the place of women and of men and of children in the social world. It is, therefore, time to take an honest look at the families that are really out there—to find the facts and, as nearly as we can, separate them from the underpinning of hidden agendas or sentimentalities. To take such a look is the way to find the moral code that is *really* taking shape. If we explore the external and internal forces shaping the family today, we shall find that families still rest firmly on some eternal truths, just as they are responding to new forces. If we are confused, it is because our understanding is superficial, not because the verities have changed.

The scandal is not that families are going to the dogs. It is that families have been abandoned by society, often most blatantly by those segments that pay lip service to it. The people who want to "save" the family are almost without exception those who would turn back the clock.

The scandal is that families are on their own, beset by violence and neglect, with divorce the only institutionalized way to deal with serious problems. Industry has been pushed only a very short way toward doing for families what it should have done all along. The welfare system breaks up one kind of family in the interest of "helping" it to become some other kind, and media images belittle family members at the same time as they push instant gratification in the name of the family.

This book was written in protest. My goal has been, as dispassionately and clearly as possible, to examine the history of families in the Western world and to compare them with other families in other parts of the world; to examine the social and psychological structure of the different kinds of families we actually find all around us; to look at what it is that keeps us from doing our family jobs better than we in fact do, whatever the particular form of family we happen to find ourselves in.

The divorce rate has been rising in what is now the United States since the 1630s. Indeed, like a bull stock market, it levels off occasionally, falls back, and then takes another jump upward. Although the divorce rate seems again to have leveled off, and may even briefly fall back, nothing points to any alteration of the overall pattern. We are not likely to see the divorce rate decline to the one that so frightened people a century ago.

But despite the dire predictions of traditionalists or the fantasies of utopians, the family will not disappear. Study after study tell us that, despite the problems, the family is thriving. Our immediate need is to turn the current family situation to a profit instead of a loss. But first we must understand what today's families actually are, objectively, not through a screen of sentimentality or pain.

The family is an evolved cultural institution built on a biological base. All animals, including human animals, have two evolved "instincts"—the instinct to reproduce and the instinct to fight for the requirements of air, water, food, shelter, and reproduction. Those instincts show up in human beings as lust (not to be confused with promiscuity) and aggression (not to be confused with violence). Many other qualities in the course of evolution have hooked onto these instincts— our capacity for intimacy on the one, our capacity for loyalty on the other. Both are fundamental to the family.

There are two principal ways of socially harnessing aggression. One is territoriality. Animals put sufficient distances between themselves to keep others under surveillance but avoid closeness. Human beings are territorial to a degree: who has not felt wariness as someone breaches our turf? We give our aggressive "instincts" the cultural forms of homes, property, nations, and armies.

The other way to harness aggression is hierarchy. Most animals can submit to an order of ranking—especially human beings. An animal such as a fox or a gibbon that has no talent for hierarchy can deal with others of its kind only by staying away. Most animals are primarily either territorial or hierarchical. Human beings are both at the same time.

There are also two main ways of socially harnessing lust to ensure both the reproduction of the species and predictable psychological rewards and social order. One is called bonding, a long-term relationship between a male and a female so that together they form a social unit. In the order of primates, to which human beings belong, most (not quite all) species that are highly territorial are also highly bonded. Gibbons, for example, do not form hierarchies; rather, a male and a female gibbon bond and live in a territory that both defend. It is this group against all others—until the young are grown, when they too become others. This looks on the surface like a human family, but the group is not part of any larger group, as human families invariably are. The human family is very different from the social forms of all other primates.

The other nonhuman way to harness sexuality to

assure social peace as well as reproduction is a looser arrangement in which a group of males, organized hierarchically, associates with a number of females (who may also be hierarchically organized), and in which the young are tended by their mothers and put up with by the males. At this opposite end of the spectrum from the gibbons is the rhesus monkey. The rhesus band is a hierarchy of males accompanied by a group of females. Females generally stay in the band in which they were born; the males, as they grow up, leave it and form peripheral groups. Some of these males, but not all, fight their way into the hierarchies of other bands so that they can reproduce. Males of the group, depending on whether the females select them and whether the other males above them in the hierarchy will put up with it, may mate with any female of the group. Chimpanzees are in between, with a loose hierarchy in which both sexes participate. Most often the females change bands, and they mate with all the male members of their new band. The males put up with and protect the young of all the females of the band, but the only family unit is the female and her young.

And human beings? We have it all ways: we are hierarchical and we do something like bonding. The difference between human bureaucracy and the "natural" hierarchy of the barnyard or the wilderness is that simple animal hierarchy is an arrangement of individuals while bureaucracy is an arrangement of roles that can be played by many different individuals. And human marriage is something like bonding. Not at all the same thing as gibbon bonding, it is cultural rather than purely genetic. That is, it is something we are taught that we can choose to do or not do, and there are many different ways to do it instead of just one genetically determined way. It primarily serves the human concept of paternity, not consciously shared by other primates. Monogamy, which is a gibbon propensity, is *not* a human one, despite the best attempts of Westerners.

The human family is so basic and so elegant that it is almost hard to understand. It is built from components found in all mammalian species. The first component is the adult female with her young, which makes up the only kind of family found among rhesus monkeys and chimpanzees. These "matrifamilies" are powerful because they can form generational chains—a daughter of one matrifamily is the mother of the next. This kind of chain is the primal linkage used by the human extended family. The second component is the adult male, who in other species (and often in our own) is primarily interested in hierarchies in which he struggles for position—the only alternative may be to live an isolated life or join a loose, peripheral group, made up only of males.

The human family arose from joining these two components. Over the millennia, when people learned about the role of the male in reproduction, they figured out that father-son relationships can be made to chain something like mother-daughter units. Father-son chains do not occur naturally. They are cultural in the sense that they spring from the idea of paternity; their purpose has to do with possessions and power. Father-son chains are not recognized among any mammals except human beings. Nevertheless, chains of males, like chains of females, underlie every human extended family. Father-daughter and mother-son relationships are recognized but, because of the sex difference, do not form chains. (There is one believe-it-or-not case in which people tried, without much success).

Then comes another cultural development: hooking the two components together by a cultural arrangement called marriage, and with it, co-parenthood. There you have both the strongest and the weakest point in the family as a system, for historically the greatest difficulty in the family has been to keep the male roped in. It still is.

There are four ways to combine the two components.

In the simplest form, one unit of each type is linked by marriage, and the monogamous family results. Another arrangement of the family components is to hook two or more female-with-young units to a single mature male. This is a polygynous family, found in many societies throughout the world, but particularly in Africa and the Middle East. It is the best means to father as many legitimate children as possible.

The two other possible forms are rare. In the first, two or more adult males can be attached to one matrifamily unit to produce the polyandrous family. Because in polyandry the males have to overlook paternity or deem it irrelevant, they are usually brothers; every husband knows that the child is close kin whether he actually begot it or not. Paternity in this kind of family is a social arrangement; the biological facts are interpreted differently. Polyandry is rare because it does not lead to the male's enhanced paternity. The last form is even rarer: two or more male units are hooked to two or more female units. This form, which approaches the rhesus monkey band, is what nineteenth-century anthropologists called group marriage. For paternity, it has all the disadvantages of polyandry, and none of the advantages of monogamy or polygyny.

Cultural development in recent years has allowed us to take a startlingly new view of those components. With the movement of women into the world outside the family, the woman and the young have come to be seen as two distinct units, which brings the total number of components to three—the adult male, the adult female, and the young. Today the children can be hooked to their mother, to their father, or to the league of both of them. This particular form was, of course, always possible, and widow(er)s and their children have always been recognized as genuine, if curtailed, family. But as these new ideas become dominant, and as the divorce rate rises, the family forms it leads to are becoming common.

The link between male and female is the weakest link

in the design of the human family. Given the importance of paternity, the link of the male to his children is often stronger than his link to a specific female. And in spite of some aberrations, the link of the female to her children is stronger than her link to any specific male, even their father. In short, the human family is based on parenthood, shared parenthood when that is feasible. We have for millennia emphasized the weak point and proceeded as if the family had been based on marriage. And we were wrong.

All of these forms of the family came into being in the dark crannies of prehistory when the males hung around and were ultimately accepted by the females. We wonder: why did they hang around? Why do they hang around? Why were they accepted? Why are they accepted? Traditionally, we assumed that the attraction was the sexual link between male and female, but today we must admit that a bonded female cannot supply anything that the nonbonded females of a band cannot supply; a bonded male cannot supply anything the nonbonded males of the band cannot supply. Most animals who live in pair-bonds are less active sexually than those outside them, and, except in a few highly repressive societies, human beings in marriage are no more sexually active than those outside marriage. The sexual activity of the bonded gibbon or orangutan male is less than that of the nonbonded baboon or rhesus or chimpanzee male, and *far* less than that of the human male.

Human males hung around—and still do—because a family makes paternity provable, and, just as important, because they grew up in families. That means that some of their most rewarding childhood experiences occurred in families, and they try to repeat them as adults. Human females accepted them—and still do—because child-rearing by two parents (and often their kin) in league is a far more efficient way of bringing up the young. However, because human beings are complex cultural creatures, they can add many other reasons for getting married: political or economic contracts between men whose sons and daughters become pawns to the contract, dependable companionship and friendship, taking fuller advantage of the special points of view of the other sex. Today older people get married for some of these same cultural reasons, and also as a result of social policy such as tax differentials and practices of insurance companies. Then there is that strange mystery called love which, as we will see in Chapter 7, is not really a mystery at all.

Today we may be faced with a movement as vital to the future of human society as that of original family formation. Just as males once opted into a family, so women today are opting into the world outside the home. It turns out that they are as good at these outside activities as men, and society will never be the same. We are undergoing a profound disruption in the family as well as in economic, political, and religious institutions. That may prove in the long run to have been the most important social result of the women's movement. The human family, then, is an intricate cultural embroidery on something that is both genetically and psychologically much more basic. And it constantly shifts with social forces.

What, then, are the social forces that shape the family, and what are the various ways the family, across the range of historical and ethnographic variation, has found to adapt to such forces? Modern society has created new and complex technological inventions and social forms from the automobile and television to political bureaucracies and new kinds of jobs that are making new demands on the family. Other institutions, such as the schools, the military, and the church, set goals for the family. How do these other institutions shape the family by supporting it, combatting it, or merely ignoring it?

In some societies—indeed, in our own less than a century ago—the family and the community were closely interlinked. Then, as a result of the vast changes in where people lived and what they did in the Industrial Age, the community changed. A hundred years ago—and in some places as recently as forty years ago—the community still had many vestiges of the peasant community in which everybody knew everybody else. That kind of face-to-face community could reward a good spouse and parent. In the days when employers lived among the people they employed, the marketplace centered on specific needs of specific people. The school in those days was also part of the community. That kind of community can never return. We are mobile; we have found other ways to make life rewarding. Common interests, not residence, lie at the basis of the new community. New kinds of links have to be forged between these new communities and our families.

For a variety of reasons, the divorce rate in the United States has gone up, and a vast service industry has emerged. Most of the people in that industry have nothing whatever to do with the quality of families. They hang on the fringes of collapsed families, providing commercial services, catering to divorce and making a profit in its aftermath. Such development of the divorce industry has not yet been accompanied by anything like equal development in a well-family industry.

But through the changes one thing is clear: there is no substitute for the family. Anything that does everything a family does is a family. Certainly some of the things that families do *can* be separated into components and each component assumed by a different institution. We could feed ourselves some other way than in family households. We could declare sexual freedom (including the freedom to choose monogamy) to be legally as well as socially recognized. We could find other ways of bequeathing our wealth. But the one thing that the family does today that cannot be done by any other existing institution is raising children. There we come face to face with the ultimate purpose of the family.

In short, it is conceivable that we can do without the family. But the family is not going to disappear because almost nobody wants it to disappear. An even stronger reason is that the family is efficient. It enables so few people to do so much, with relatively little social energy, for so many. The family may not always, or even often, do all those things very well, but it does them. The real question is how to make it more effective and more rewarding.

In some ages, the family seems to lose a little of its centrality. Today is such a time. The purposes to which the family is put can change: in seventeenth-century England the family was largely an institution that controlled property, including access to jobs; by the late nineteenth and early twentieth century, it had become primarily an institution for raising children. The proportion of individuals who do not get involved in families may change from one era to the next—it is higher today than it was a few decades ago.

When most of us worry about the family, we are not really worried about whether any family will survive, but rather whether some particular form of it will. The answer to the first question—will the family survive?—is almost certainly yes. The answer to the second—will the particular form of the family that I value survive?—is probably no. Because when there is a change in the social context—the environment—in which families find themselves, the families have to change in response. This is one fundamental problem that this book addresses. The other problem is how understanding family processes can make all forms of the family more rewarding, so that we can raise better-equipped kids and find the most peace, fun, and trust.

Part I

The Divorce Industry

1

The Divorce
Industry

The first-recorded divorce in the United States occurred in Plymouth Colony soon after its establishment. The number of divorces has been rising ever since—falling back occasionally, then mounting again. By 1804, one marriage in 100 ended in divorce (at least in Connecticut). At the end of the 1920s, it was one marriage in six. By 1980, divorce had become so common—one marriage in two or three, depending on how you count—that thousands of people clustered around divorcing families. Lawyers, therapists, and detectives all hang on the fringe of collapsed families, providing services and usually making a profit. All kinds of other businesses also profit from divorce: from landlords who provide a location for a second household to greeting card companies, from real estate agents who sell houses that would not be on the market without divorces to automobile manufacturers and oil companies and airlines that provide transportation between the two new households. Public servants like judges and bailiffs and social workers and clerks in the public service and welfare offices are kept busy.

These people, except for the therapists and clergy, have little professional regard for the quality of families; they are involved in divorce. When it became apparent in the 1960s that merely "saving" most rocky marriages was vain and misguided, we put our energy into "creative'' divorce rather than into a well-family industry. In spite of the efforts of many family service agencies, most families still get help only when they are in trouble. As far as anyone has yet figured out, a well-family industry isn't as profitable as a divorce industry. So services to one-parent families or stepfamilies run from scarce to nonexistent.

This immense new divorce industry has grown up silently around us. Because nobody keeps records this way, it is impossible even to estimate either the size of the industry or its annual cash flow, but a little thought will convince you that it is as big as the automobile industry. It and its products affect the lives of as many people. But, since it does not get into labor disputes or national statistics, and is not the subject of television jingles, we haven't noticed.

The analogy to the automobile industry can be carried further. That industry is dependent on many other industries, the biggest of which are petroleum and steel. The three link intricately into a megaindustry, with all sorts of appendages: manufacturers of rubber tires, upholstery, mirrors, and chrome, not to mention people who make, sell, and service cars. The emergence of this immense, coordinated industry was one of the most important developments in the economic history of the early twentieth century.

The divorce industry too is an amalgam of other industries and professions, and certainly it is one of the most important developments of the social history of the twentieth century. It lacks a vast network of factories and sales rooms and fueling stations, but hundreds of thousands of people are involved in the divorce industry at thousands of sites.

The nodes in the complex divorce industry network—the places where the various services join together or where people meet to do the business connected with divorce—are often intimate and kept out of sight. Sometimes the participants are actively hostile to one another—not competitive like General Motors and

Ford, but hostile in the sense that some therapists think lawyers damage their clients, while many lawyers think detectives are unnecessary to *their* clients. Nevertheless, a broader view indicates that all these supporting networks behind the divorce industry work together because they need each other.

There is a lot of money to be made in the divorce industry. Getting divorced isn't cheap: the lawyers, the therapists, the detectives, the accountants get paid directly and well by the clients. Helpful clergy are also paid directly, if less well. Taxes pay for the courts, judges, bailiffs, and court reporters, and also for the district attorneys' staff who collect the child support checks from delinquent fathers and for the welfare workers and checks on which some divorced families depend.

Other people make good livings in supporting services that we don't think much about. Greeting card companies market "congratulations on your divorce" cards on the same racks as wedding anniversary cards and birthday cards; airlines haul unaccompanied children back and forth for visitations, at adult fares. Neither business depends on divorce for its existence, but both profit from it.

The divorce industry is booming. Social scientists and journalists—and, indeed, divorcees themselves—churn out articles and books. That involves not just the writers, but editors, subsidiary rights staff (to sell serial and reprint and television rights), printers, distributors, bookstores. It matters little that many of those articles and books are not very informative, for there are still areas of the divorce experience and its aftermath about which we know very little.

The subject of divorce is a mainstay of today's entertainment industry. Script writers and actors and technicians, the movie studios and the networks, as well as the sponsors and advertising agencies, get in the act. And as spectators, we are *all* involved in the divorce industry, even if we don't make any money off it.

The legal profession lies at the heart of the divorce

industry. There are today over 660,000 lawyers. Until recent years, most lawyers took divorce cases. However, divorce practice is now becoming ever more specialized.

Laws about marriage and divorce are part of family law, and the lawyers who specialize in them are called "matrimonial lawyers" (which usually means that they specialize in divorce). Most state and local bar associations have branches devoted to family law. There is even a group that calls itself the American Academy of Matrimonial Lawyers, a professional association whose members meet twice a year for almost a week, thereby giving business to the hotel and resort industry, and again to the airlines. These matrimonial lawyers discuss their mutual problems and learn from one another through comparison of cases and of problems that confront colleagues in other states. They also listen to lectures from economists, from accountants and tax experts, from psychologists—and sometimes even from anthropologists.

Family law firms have grown in the last two decades, while the individual practitioner is dying out, certainly in urban areas. A woman now in her seventies who has been practicing family law in San Francisco for many years told me, "Every successful family lawyer has founded a firm so that more people can ride on the reputation made by the senior partner. That way, they can churn out a lot more money." She adds that the real difficulty with this new situation is that she now has to work with a lot of young incompetents. She summed it up: "It is far more bureaucratized. But the balance sheet is very positive."

Probably even more important, the competence requirements for matrimonial lawyers have risen. In the old days, any lawyer could put together a simple divorce case. Today simple cases no longer require lawyers; self-help is enough. But the cases that do go through lawyers demand that the attorneys know such recondite areas as tax and real estate law. Furthermore, in order to do their jobs well, they must be accomplished in many areas that used to be far beyond the law: they have to know about such things as psychotherapy. "Fifteen years ago," my trusted woman lawyer friend told me, "lawyers all thought only crazy people went to psychiatrists. Today almost all of them know better, and some of them are even willing to put clients into touch with therapists they know and trust."

Today matrimonial lawyers are even using complex econometrics to compute standards of living and to make projections about them. Accountants are hired to run out budgets and income divisions and cash flow and asset management on their microcomputers. Many matrimonial lawyers are also seriously concerned about (but, as far as I could discover, have not found much to do about) the social implications of their profession and the impact of so much divorce on the community. They are far better informed on such matters as family theory than they were twenty years ago.

Specializations in marriage and divorce law abound. Many matrimonial lawyers, for example, will not handle contested custody cases. They call in specialists. Even within that specialty, subspecialties are emerging: those who do nothing but appeals, those who work with both parents (something the legal profession, dedicated as it is to clarifying the rights of each litigant through the adversary process, traditionally has branded unethical), those who specialize in representing the child's position. However, "I just run a general family practice," one lawyer told me. "I don't worry about whether we are handling a lesbian mother or some other unusual kind of thing. I can handle it." But that lawyer does nothing but divorces and it was not very many years ago when divorce itself was not a specialty. The general lawyer in the old days—the early 1960s—could say, "Oh, sure. Divorces aren't difficult. I do one now and then." That attitude is about gone, and the general family lawyer is going.

The women's movement has also had an immense

impact on the practice of family law. Today in many areas—Chicago and San Francisco, for example—women make up a quarter of the lawyers in the courtroom. Attorneys, both men and women, expect the proportion to continue to rise right along with the higher proportion of women being accepted into law schools. Many wives seeking divorce—and no few husbands—prefer women attorneys. They are said to take more time, to listen better to the client's view of the break-up, and to be more sympathetic, wishing to create good solutions rather than merely to apply the law. "Twenty years ago," one male Chicago attorney said, "women worried about having a woman attorney—they were afraid the court wouldn't listen to her. But that has long since proved wrong. The women's movement has changed all that."

This rise of woman attorneys is only part of a more general change: in the old days of less than two decades ago, most wives in divorce actions were homemakers. But two forces altered that. Chronic inflation, making it impossible for many families to live on one salary, gave more women the excuse to leave their homes (or, for some women, forced them to do so) and make use of whatever education they had. Second, the women's movement radically changed women's expectations, and made them less willing to put up with humiliation and violence than were their mothers. But on the other side of the coin, a wife is no longer "protected" when she appears in court. She is evaluated in pretty much the same way a husband is: what are his or her achievements, potential, and responsibilities? Since it is now expected that she will work, the judge can ask how much financial responsibility is reasonable to expect her to take on at the same time that he asks how much the husband should. Thus, in the divorce action itself, the irrelevance of the attorney's sex is echoed by the lesser importance of the client's sex.

Men have changed their ideas and their attitudes about themselves as well as about women. More than anything else, male attitudes about the family and about being a father have changed. As a Chicago judge put it: "Men have got over feeling sissy about wanting to bring up their own kids. Men are winning up to sixty percent of contested custody cases, probably because most men still do not bring such a case without very good reason." In the middle 1960s, most men would not go through the painful and dirty shenanigans that were then necessary to win custody (they had to prove the mothers "unfit" as mothers), even if they had good reasons for wanting it, and even if "the best interests of the child" might have dictated it. My attorney friend remarked, "People still come to me. They remember that not very many years ago I was the only lawyer in this city who could consistently win paternal custody cases."

Money matters have changed in the last twenty years far more than most of us realize. Inflation has meant that a lot more divorces involve property of far greater face value. A middle-class divorce no longer involves only a car, a television set, a dog, and an $8000 equity in a house. That same house is now worth more than $150,000, *far* more than many industrial claims or tort actions. Divorce lawyers are involved in the control and redistribution of a lot of money.

As a result of all these changes, the last twenty years have seen a vast improvement in the social rank and position of matrimonial lawyers. The status totem pole of the legal profession is covertly computed on the basis of how much money the lawyer makes, the law school attended, the skill of the lawyer, the kind of office he or she keeps, the kind of cases he takes, how many she wins. Another criterion in the ranking of lawyers— though most lawyers don't recognize it in this form—is the amount of emotion they have to deal with. Corporations have no emotions, so all other things being equal, corporation lawyers rank at the top. Criminals have little else, and, with some famous exceptions, criminal lawyers rank at the bottom of the heap.

In the old days, 1964, divorce lawyers ranked only

just above the criminal lawyers. Today their status has gone up. The main reason is that divorce, even with no-fault, has become legally much more complicated as more and more laws are passed to protect the rights of the divorcing parties and their children. The other reason is that divorce is not as messy as it used to be. Since the advent of no-fault, less perjury is required, and fewer histrionics. The social disapproval of divorce is not as overwhelming as it once was, and matrimonial lawyers have a slightly less tawdry image.

Matrimonial lawyers are often portrayed as the bad guys of the divorce industry. Divorcing people tell horror stories about the ineptitude or deceit of their lawyers. And sometimes they are right. But more often the lawyer is a scapegoat; a target for the immense rage of divorcing people, at whom they can aim the venom actually generated in other relationships, or at whom they can rail as a sort of depersonalized fate. Lawyers are called "grasping," which probably means no more than that they work by the hour, and their services are expensive. They are called calculating and heartless because, as they themselves admit, they are not adequately equipped to be therapists. Lawyers are more accurately seen as fall guys of the divorcing partners than as bad guys of the divorce drama.

Judges are major actors in that drama. Indeed, they, more than anyone else, seem to me to be the "good guys" of the industry—an attitude I certainly did not hold in the early 1960s. Their number is large, there are over 30 judges hearing divorce actions in the courts of Chicago alone.

The attitude of matrimonial court judges toward their work has also changed markedly in the last twenty years. Judges in those days were far less well informed about the psychological dimensions of marriage, divorce, and custody. As a result, they saw only foolish and vindictive wives, cruel husbands and irresponsible fathers, unprepared and grasping lawyers. The articles they were publishing in the law journals in the years around 1960 reveal just how primitive (by today's standards) the views of marriage and divorce were. Certainly the present generation of law journal editors would not publish them.

To see how far we have come, take a look at a judge's statement that appeared in the *Florida Bar Journal* in 1963: "As we stride into the hearing room, we see the ever-present domestic triangle: the lawyer, the client, the mother. . . . The case is simple and the decree pro confesso against the husband makes it even simpler. The terrible things he did might not be believable when heard from the lips of that quiet little angel, but cannot be doubted when repeated at length by the mother who knew all along what a deadbeat the defendant was. In ten minutes time the final decree is signed and another female has completed the married at 17, baby at 18, divorced at 19 ritual. . . . Off to a fine start! After all, what else could we do on the basis of the evidence before us? Deny the divorce after hearing the girl's mother testify or award the child to the absent (that is, unrepresented in court) father or cut the support on a stab-in-the-dark basis? Of course not, we had no choice. Who's next?"

That particular judge also "understood" the ex-husband/fathers only in terms of his stereotypes and prejudices: "Yes, he knows he is behind in his payments. Yes, he knows he must keep up the mortgage on the house. 'But judge, I haven't had steady work. I've paid what I could.' . . . We find the man in contempt, provide that he may purge himself by making up past-due payments within thirty days, award a reasonable fee to the lawyer, and sit back with the full knowledge that next month we will have to put the man in jail for failing to obey this month's order. Pass quickly to the next case—it may give us room for discretion."

The combination of insight and scorn for what he is doing is typical of judges of that era. The reason—

besides what we can see as his obvious contempt for women and identification with the husband—is that in those days it really was a far dirtier job than it is now.

Many judges in the early 1960s found this combination of perjury, deceitfulness, and raw emotion almost unbearable. Because they could not point accurately to their true concern, they complained about unprepared lawyers and silly or vindictive clients. They considered their assignment at best a sort of judicial Siberia, at worst the seventh circle of hell. They longed for the day when they could get back to interesting torts and decent contracts. They were rotated quickly in and out of the domestic relations courts so that every judge would have to do his turn.

By the early 1980s, the judges' views were dramatically different. As one judge put it: "What I do is important. The future of families and of children depends on what I do. Is it reasonable to spend a week on a liability suit that involves $50,000 and rush through a divorce action in which not only is the property worth a quarter of a million, but the futures of three children are at stake?"

Although the domestic court is still unpopular among some judges—and it may depend on the law in their particular jurisdiction as much as anything else— other areas are fortunate in having conscientious judges who have come to know a lot about domestic relations. A few even fight against transfer to another division—an attitude that would have been unthinkable two decades earlier.

Thus, although inflation produced some important changes in what happens when we divorce, most of the improvement seems to have been created by no-fault legislation on the one hand and the new way in which society looks at families and at divorce on the other. The divorces in which no property or custody are involved no longer clog the court calendars in many states, they can be done by simply filing papers with the clerk.

Thus, the cases that actually take up the court's time are more likely to involve substantial property settlements and, even more vital, the future of children. Neither of these types of cases *must* come before a judge in many states, but it is the opinion of lawyers and judges that most of them do, even when (as in a large proportion of them) the principals do not make a court appearance.

And perhaps even more important, in all states except two (Illinois and South Dakota), judges no longer need play out the charade of establishing "marital fault" that so often under the old law bordered on—or crossed over into—perjury. They don't have to make decisions about who was at fault on the basis of stereotyped or rigged evidence. They don't have to listen to the baleful woes and the spiteful wrongs that messed up the marriage. When disputants come into their courts, they are fighting over property, not finding fault with one another or setting out to prove who did what to whom. Whatever it may mean for the divorcing husband and wife, for judges and lawyers it is "nicer."

Judges in the 1980s are likely to say that they are glad to be rid of the adversary system in family cases. Donald King, one of the most respected judges in San Francisco, told me that the adversary system works well for litigation such as automobile accidents or contracts, because the contestants need never see one another again, but in child custody cases, the adversary system makes it even more difficult for the parents to communicate afterward.

He went on to say that the adversary system may provide a legal result in a custody dispute, but it seldom solves the underlying problems, and may even add to them. "It is absolutely absurd for parents to turn to a judge who has little skill or knowledge in the area of parent-child relationships, knows little psychology, and never even gets a chance to see the children except for a few minutes under the very worst possible circumstances. It is a terrible abrogation of their parental rights and obligations to turn any of that over to a judge. If they can't do it, we ought to help them, not take the responsibility away from them. The best way to resolve the problems is to teach people who are getting divorced that although their relationship as husband and wife is ending, their newly organized and separate family is just beginning.''

Now judges in the domestic relations courts of California meet every year to discuss the specific problems of their job. They get training in many esoteric subjects far beyond the traditional legal requirements bearing on matrimonial cases. Judge King of San Francisco exemplifies the new attitude; in Hawaii Judge Betty Vitusek has turned the domestic relations court into not merely an honorable pursuit but the home of significant research. In Chicago Judge Charles Fleck finds the old attitude turned absolutely around.

Today, many therapists specialize in seeing people through the divorce process, while others deal primarily with postdivorce problems. Still others work with stepfamilies or with children of divorce and remarriage, sometimes even specializing in children of specific age groups. We see not only a growth in the psychotherapy industry, but also an immense branching into specialization.

Psychiatrists now fill out medical insurance forms of the patients who consult them at the time of divorce with the diagnosis, "crisis of adult development." Many of them see their task as helping the patient to rebuild the self-esteem that first a miserable marriage, and then the legal and social pressures of divorce itself, sometimes destroy. They help people discover their actual options—an amazing number of divorcing people need this kind of help because they do not know that options exist and have never pictured themselves pursuing choices other than the ones they made years before.

Many counties now have staffs of counselors attached to some courts—clinical psychologists and social workers—who discuss options with both the divorcing parents, preferably together, so they can themselves make their own custody arrangements. They encourage both parents to fulfill their obligations, continue to take an interest in the children's development, and to get at least some of the rewards of parenting. These counselors believe that arrangements made in this way—especially if the children themselves are present to hear at least some parts of it—are much better carried out by the parents than those dictated by a judge. Best of all, such parents can consider their own decisions in a settlement as a pledge made directly to the children.

But lawyers, judges, and psychotherapists are certainly not the only professionals to get involved in the new, far more complex institutions of divorce. The real estate industry would shrivel if the divorce rate suddenly collapsed. In the states that have community property laws, realtors with whom I have discussed the matter estimate that as many as a fourth of the houses on the market are put there to settle claims made at the time of divorce. (Lawyers, judges, and psychotherapists are skeptical of such figures.)

In those states without community property laws, called the "common law states," there is either a tendency toward or laws demanding what is called "equitable division" of property. However, in most of those states, the law does not say just what such an equitable division might be, so it is up to the lawyers to "prove" one. Litigation in this matter has all but replaced litigation about fault. Both the attorneys and the courts fall back on many different kinds of specialists and experts. There is, for example, a new breed of economist who specializes in creating plans for "equitable" financial settlements that will alter the style of living of the family members as little as possible, at least from the standpoint of the spouse whose attorney hires the economist. They use fancy mathematical models and econometrics and do "projections" based on formulas that take into consideration the work histories and potential earning power of the spouses, the cost of retraining previously nonemployed wives for jobs, and the estimated costs of education of the children. They adjust and readjust all these real and potential resources and come out with recommendations.

In "common law" states, the real estate industry may be almost as deeply involved in the divorce industry as it is in community property states, although my information is not as secure. It would seem that many people *want* to move at the time of divorce, so that the property is sold in the interests of "equable distribution." In Virginia, for example, real estate agents gave me the same range of figures that they provide in California. The so-called "mingled" households of today are sometimes seriously upset by divorce. In such households, two or more couples "mingle" to buy a house that neither could afford alone. They fix it up so that two families—or at least two couples—can have a modicum of privacy as well as some "mingled" living. Then, one of the couples splits. The other couple can't afford to buy them out so another big house goes on the market.

The real estate business feels the influence of divorce in yet another way: an intelligent woman with no special training or experience, but with the right kind of personality, may succeed at selling real estate far beyond her expectations in most other fields. An immense number of "real estate ladies" went into that business at the time of their divorces.

The private investigation industry—part of the divorce industry from its earliest days—has been immensely affected by no-fault divorce laws and by the emergence of new divorce practices. Private investigators, in the days before no-fault divorce, spent a lot of time lurking to collect nasty facts on the clandestine activities of the person whom divorcees call "my ex-to-be." If fault could be proved, the divorce was more readily granted, or the conditions of support and alimony altered. If a paying spouse could "prove something" in court, lower or higher alimony payments were ordered. Custody changes could be demanded on the "proved immorality" of a parent. If a woman's ex-husband's detective found out that her lover spent the night, the ex-husband could either reduce his payments or scare her into doing whatever he wished on the threat of cutting off support or removing the children. Seldom is that true any longer, except in Illinois where a 1980 Supreme Court decision gave custody of three daughters to a father they did not want to live with on the grounds that their mother was in an apparently stable live-in arrangement with another man.

A highly respected matrimonial lawyer told me that the old use of detectives to establish grounds was a silly game, and described a case in which a detective came back to his client saying that his ex-to-be was doing exactly what she had reported to him: going to church meetings. So a different detective was put on the job and found that the wife was having an affair with the first detective, while the husband was paying the detective's fee as expenses of the case. "We won that one," the attorney summed it up.

Private investigators assure me that the total amount of time they give to family matters has not dropped as a result of the new no-fault laws. Rather, new specialties have appeared. For several detective agencies in both northern and southern California, "family business" supplies about 30 percent of their total activities. But instead of hokey-pokey, the detectives are now tracking down money or property squirreled away in hopes that it will not be discovered when the property settlement is made. As one attorney explained it, "Today I use detectives mostly to find hidden bank accounts."

An entirely new specialty has emerged—the investigative auditor. He or she is an accountant whose task is to trace all of a person's assets, however hidden. The bulk of their clients are people in the process of divorce. Primarily these clients are women, because men are more likely to hide assets than women. The task of the investigative auditor is made easier by the fact that most people who hide money rarely begin to do it until three or four years before the divorce, hence their trails are fresh.

In addition, detectives' business is fueled by a vast increase in child kidnappings. My helpful attorney said, "The best detectives take a lot of time with kidnappings. However, I myself won't take on those cases any more. They are exhausting and, after all, I'm over seventy."

It is not a crime for a parent to take a child away. However, if the court has named the other parent as the custodial parent, the kidnapper is in defiance of that court order, and thus may become criminally liable. The number of parents kidnapping their own children has risen dramatically, a phenomenon that will be discussed at some length in Chapter 9. Along with this increase, the number of private investigators who devote a major proportion of their time to tracing "kidnapped" children and providing assistance for the custodial parents to "rekidnap" has risen. Each big agency has one or more such specialists.

The reason that people turn to private detectives for these purposes is simple. As one detective explained: "The police departments only find kidnapped kids on a fluke. A guy gets stopped for a traffic ticket and they check it and find out he is wanted on a child-stealing charge. But nobody is putting in any exhaustive time and effort looking for the kid. They have far too much to do already. That is where we come in."

This kind and public-spirited man (who got his training as an investigator in the military during World War II) went on: "We don't have a good parent locator in this country. The FBI says that if they got these cases, they wouldn't have time to do anything else. The whole thing is difficult because the law enforcement people don't have time to do the cases right, and we private investigators don't have access to the kinds of records they can get: social security, IRS, the whole number. We can't get to them. So, there really isn't *anybody* set up to do this job efficiently.''

The average cost of a successful "rekidnapping" among the seven investigators I talked with was $14,000 in 1980–1981. Many investigations are never completed because the custodial parent runs out of money, fewer because the investigator cannot trace the child.

There is still a small, residual business for private investigators among people who were divorced under the old system and are stuck with high alimony payments. One detective told me, "We still do some investigations on cohabitation—some men can still get out of alimony that way. You can reduce or knock out the support from the ex-husband if she is living with another man."

There is, moreover, a small number of older women who, every few months, get a detective to run down what their former husbands are up to. When I asked the head of one large agency what they did with this information, he replied, "Nothing. They don't want to do anything. They just want to know." For reasons that this investigator could not even guess, a male client had never made this kind of request about the activities of his former wife.

The divorce industry shows up at petty levels as well. Some people take old wedding and family photographs to airbrush specialists in order to have ex-spouses, ex-in-laws, or other people expunged. The cost is a lot higher, but you can also have somebody else brushed in—picture of the "immigrant" is pasted on, the edges airbrushed so that they don't show, and the whole is rephotographed.

Some wedding photographers offer, as a special service, personalized albums for each of the wedding guests. I know a young woman whose mother begged her not to invite her father's wife to her wedding. The bride replied that she could not do that—her stepmother had been married to her father for over ten years and simply could not be ignored (she spared her mother the statement that she was, in any case, fond of her stepmother and grateful to her on many counts). The mother, she said gently, would simply have to bear up. However, when the album of photographs prepared for the bride's mother was delivered, the stepmother had thoughtfully been removed from all the pictures. And her mother (said the bride) did not even realize it.

There are a lot of other minor characters in the divorce industry: diet centers, gymnasiums, employment bureaus, travel agencies, financial advisors. And let's not leave out the people who own and tend the bars. It is not just professionals and entrepreneurs who are involved in the divorce industry. Well-meaning amateurs also get in the act. In 1960, the most powerful support group for single parents, made up largely of the newly divorced, was Parents Without Partners. That organization was founded in the 1950s to offer support and instruction to divorced, widowed, or never married parents of young children. Later in what divorcees in those days called "the process," it became for many of them a dependable and comfortable social group. P.W.P. offered a variety of social activities in which the children of these divorced people could meet and play. It incidentally—and, in spite of what some detractors said, secondarily—formed a dating league long before the days of computer dating services.

When I studied divorce in the Bay Area of California in 1963, I found a number of active, indeed vital, chapters of Parents Without Partners there. People were excited about the new activities and programs through which they could help one another. One of them was the "S.O.S." program, developed by a young woman named Sally Spray. It established lectures and discussion groups to educate newly divorced people in their rights, in regaining their self-respect and social poise, and coping with their children. S.O.S. was taken over by the national organization of P.W.P. Every chapter of the organization got a how-to-do-it kit.

By 1980, the picture had changed dramatically. By then the local newspaper, every Friday, listed over 30 special service and limited-interest organizations for divorcees in the one Bay Area community on which I had focused my original research. P.W.P. was still listed, but it was now smaller, its members older, complaining that they could not recruit new members. They told me that the national organization of Parents Without Partners had been sued so many times that the insurance policies of the central organization required that they cut back the number of open houses—their main recruiting device—they could have each year. Certainly the generalized services offered by P.W.P. are not in demand to the extent they were in earlier days. Rather, groups organized around specific interests have emerged and gone into the singles business for themselves. New kinds of support groups have burgeoned along with the divorce rate. Although divorce is undoubtedly just as difficult an emotional experience in the 1980s as it ever was, people today are far better served by support groups, catering to far more diverse interests. The Sierra Club and most churches, for example, have singles groups in that community. There are singles bridge clubs and singles skiing clubs. Singles groups may be made up of people whose special interests are movies or health food or any number of other hobbies or activities. Body exchanges are far more numerous and open about their purpose.

The economic dimensions of this much divorce can be fathomed by realizing that to run two households instead of one means two rent checks, two light bills, two fuel bills, two telephones. That puts the landlords and the utility companies on the fringes of the divorce industry. Somebody has to pay all those lawyers, all those therapists, all those investigators, indeed, all those airbrush artists. And every time the house turns over, the realtor gets 6 percent. Divorce on this scale means a redistribution of an amount of wealth that would, in a few years, seem to challenge the national debt.

The most vital part of the divorce industry is the experience of the principal players in the drama: fathers and mothers, sons and daughters, grandparents and stepparents. Much of the rest of this book is about them, and about the families they form.

It cannot be said too many times that divorce and the divorce industry, no matter what we think of them, cannot create unsatisfactory marriages. The problem is not divorce—the problem is miserable marriages.

The divorce industry will not disappear. The solution is a well-family industry. That is what the final chapter of the book is about. The beginnings of a well-family industry are to be found in wide public recognition of the fact that there are many kinds of family out there, and we really *can* do them all well!

2

A Short History of Marriage and Divorce in the Western World

The history of marriage and divorce furnishes a record of the way other institutions have pulled families back and forth over time. Marriage in most societies is used to control and give expression to sexuality, but the values such control serves and the kind of demands that are to be controlled vary. Marriage and the family are also found in many places to cement relationships not just between families but also between larger social groups. The relationship between the family and religion is often complex. In parts of India and Africa before contact with Europe, the family, usually represented by its ancestors, was the object of worship. In the West, the family was often said to be an undergirding of the Church, thus giving the Church an excuse for its strict control over the family. The family has also been said in many societies—and at many stages in the history of the West—to be the major social unit underpinning the state. That is, the state is made up of families, and the royal family or the "first family" was both a component and the symbol of the state.

Almost everywhere—although the family is universally recognized, there are a few believe-it-or-not exceptions—the family organizes the cooperative efforts of adults and children and gives them a framework. The members of a family are a remarkably efficient unit for carrying out some of the most important tasks of society. We have come to expect the family, in the process, to provide relationships in which trust can grow. It is the modern view that if the family does all this, adults can achieve contentment and children their best development.

The institutions of marriage and divorce as we know them in the West derive from the ancient Semites, particularly the Israelites on the one hand, and the classical Greeks on the other. The history of marriage and divorce in the West falls into three periods. The ancient period, before the Christian Church took over responsibility for family institutions, can be dated from earliest times to A.D. 305. The second period is that in which marriage and divorce were controlled completely by the Church; it runs from 305 to 1534, when the Act of Supremacy created the Church of England. The third period—the period of marriage and divorce by civil law—extends from 1534 to the present.

Several premises underlie this story. Their occasional conflicts provide a framework within which people argue about the family. In one view, marriage is assumed to be something like a contract. The contract between husband and wife may be extended to, or even replaced by, a contract between two families. Another way of looking at marriage has run through history as a sort of *Doppelganger*: marriage as a relationship that is its own reward. Those two ideas of the inner nature of marriage are still found today: one that a good relationship makes the marriage, the other that a publicly recognized contract or sacrament makes the marriage. From one perspective, marriage is a private matter; from the other, it is public. The two views have struggled for centuries and the struggle still goes on.

Another premise underlying the Western family is that just as marriage can be seen as a contract, so the parent, especially the father, has rights in children of a kind that are very like rights in property. English Common Law is redolent of this assumption. Today we are only just beginning to be able to question the last premise: if the Church or the State controls the family, it traditionally has done so by controlling marriage and divorce. Until very recently it had never occurred to anyone that the view of parenthood as ownership of children could be altered to a loving view. We can today as never before ask whether legal and religious control of parenting is not wiser and more profitable in the long run than trying to control parenting by controlling marriage and divorce.

The ancient Hebrews looked upon the family primarily as a means to control sexuality and to bring the individual under the blanket of religion. Power within the marriage relationship itself lay almost entirely with the husband, although his family—particularly his father and father's brothers—had some control over his actions. The husband had "power of life and death" over wife and children, and in some periods the law backed him up when he exercised it. Men could sacrifice their children, sell them into slavery, or use them as pawns in their own economic activities, and arranged their marriages.

This power was backed by religious prescription as well as obligation. The father was not only the protector of the family, but also the priest in all family religious services. In that dual role, he could demand obedience from all. Part of a man's religious obligation was to marry to provide heirs, not only for his worldly goods, but also to carry out after his death rituals that would assure both his place in history and continuity of the tribes of Israel, themselves lineage organizations closely associated with family.

In this patriarchal society, the duty of a woman was

37

to obey her husband. The duty of children to their father was second only to their duty to God. A man could divorce his wife readily and easily. The basic law of divorce among the ancient Semites is contained in Deuteronomy:

> When a man hath taken a wife, and married
> her, and it come to pass that she find no favor
> in his eyes, because he hath found some
> uncleanness in her: then let him write her a
> bill of divorcement, and give it in her hand,
> and send her out of his house. And when she
> is departed out of his house, she may go and
> be another man's wife.

Centuries of haggling followed, as one attempt followed another to delineate precisely what "unclean" meant. Literally, the original Hebrew word means "nakedness in any particular quality." Even before the Christian Era began, some asserted that adultery was the only meaning; others claimed just as vehemently that the idea should apply much more widely. The scholar Hillel, a few years before the birth of Christ, said that even bad cooking was enough. And still others said that merely finding somebody more beautiful made the wife "unclean." However, an ancient Hebrew could not divorce his wife if he had had a sexual relationship with her before marriage, or if he accused her falsely of unchastity.

The ancient Jewish "bill of divorcement" was a document called a *get*, written by a scribe. Not until the first century A.D. did the wife win the right to contest the *get* before a special court; but even then she had no recourse if the court agreed with the husband.

The ancient Greeks and Romans, on the other hand, looked upon marriage primarily as a means to cement social relationships between families and to maintain the class system. The husband/father in ancient Greece, as among the Hebrews, had almost unlimited power over his wife and children. Again, it was every man's obligation to marry. Indeed, under the laws of Solon in the sixth century B.C., what we today would call a "never-married" man could be prosecuted by the civil authorities. Greek wives were in some senses chattels. Rights in a wife could, for example, be property. Women were cloistered and kept from the view of outsiders.

Greek marriage was a matter of contract between the males of the husband's family and the wife's. Divorce was possible from the first, but heavy fines were levied on the husband if a divorce was considered capricious. A divorced wife could leave with her dowry and the results of her own labor. It was theoretically possible, but in practice difficult, for a woman to bring a divorce action. She had to get out of her quarters and make her way to the court with a written statement. We have few cases, but we do know that Alcibiades had a wife named Hipparete who tried to file a divorce petition. Her husband got together a gang of men who dragged her forcibly out of the court.

Roman law had an immense and direct impact on our own legal institutions. The Romans looked on marriage as a private arrangement between families, with neither law nor religion having anything to do with it. Roman courts were concerned only if there were property rights involved. Like Greek marriage, Roman marriage was contracted between males—a man could contract the marriage of his daughter or sister. Theoretically he had to have her permission, but since most brides were girls of 12, that permission, in most cases, probably was more formal than actual.

Patrician Roman men, like the ancient Semites and Greeks, were under an obligation to marry—in fact, to marry patrician women—in a ceremony carried out in the presence of ten witnesses. This kind of marriage was called *conferreateo*. The wife passed from the "palm" of her father—signifying political control—to the palm of her husband. If he was not himself a family head, she was declared subject to his family head instead of to her own. If she owned property or had a dowry from her family, full title to it passed immediately to the husband. A wife could be divorced by a ceremony that precisely undid what was done by the wedding ceremony. However, the husband's rights to divorce were strictly limited and controlled, and he had to have the permission of his family council. Divorce was apparently very rare in this kind of marriage. The wife had far more freedom than a Greek wife had. However, Saint Monica, the mother of Saint Augustine, told Roman wives: "Take control of your tongue. It is the duty of servants to obey their master. . . . You have made a contract of servitude."

About 500 B.C. the plebian classes of Rome also got the right to contract formal marriages. Their unions were called *coemptio,* a form of bridewealth marriage whereby the husband gave the bride's family a piece of copper called the *rausdusculum* in return for rights in her and in the children she bore. Giving the copper indicated the husband's group's willingness to take legal responsiblity for the woman. Its acceptance signified her family's willingness to forego such responsibility. In other forms of marriage no control over the bride passed to her husband's family; she had to spend three nights a year away from his home to symbolize her position of freedom, else she passed into the palm of her husband and his household head. Marriage by coemption could also be dissolved. The husband merely repudiated his wife and gave up the power over her that he had acquired at the wedding.

As distinctions between patricians and plebes, between citizens and noncitizens, gradually diminished in Rome, a form of marriage called *jurum matrimonium* evolved. In that form, no one gained power over the woman. These marriages depended *only* on the parties continuing to live together. Divorce was often obtained for old age, barrenness, ill health, military service, or desertion.

Marriage and divorce "reform" came about with Julius Caesar. His code imposed fines on both spouses for divorce. A husband could keep a sixth of his wife's dowry if he divorced her for adultery. If he committed adultery, he had to return the entire dowry to the wife's family. In imperial Rome, something very like "grounds" for divorce came into existence. A husband could divorce his wife for adultery, preparing poison, acting as a procuress; a wife could divorce a murderer or a man who prepared poisons or robbed tombs. If a man divorced a woman capriciously, she could demand not only her own dowry, but that of his next wife.

After this time, the marriage law of Rome came more and more under the aegis of the Christian Church. The early Christian concern with morality in sex, and hence the family, was paramount. Although ecclesiastic controversy about divorce is much older, the Council of Elvira in 305 marks the beginning of the period of Church control when the Roman Church laid down its first rules about marriage. The ideas behind the rules, however, were very much older. The basis of the Christian position on divorce comes from the book of Matthew in the New Testament. It is told that a Pharisee asked Jesus about divorcing a wife, a subject hotly disputed by the scholars of the day.

> And he answered and said unto them,
> Have ye not read, that he which made them at
> the beginning made them male and female,
> And said, For this cause shall a man leave
> his father and mother, and shall cleave unto
> his wife: and they twain shall be one flesh?
> Wherefore they are no more twain, but one
> flesh. What therefore God hath joined
> together, let not man put asunder.
> They say unto him, Why did Moses then
> command to give a writing of divorcement,
> and put her away? . . .
> And I say unto you, Whosoever shall put

> away his wife, except it be for fornication, and
> shall marry another, committeth adultery: and
> whoso marrieth her which is put away doth
> commit adultery.

This statement became the cornerstone of the Christian position, but was subject to many different interpretations. For example, St. Paul in the first book of Corinthians complicated things further:

> It is good for a man not to touch a woman.
> Nevertheless, to avoid fornication, let
> every man have his own wife, and let every
> woman have her own husband.
> Let the husband render unto the wife due
> benevolence: and likewise also the wife unto
> the husband. . . .
> I say therefore to the unmarried and
> widows, It is good for them if they abide even
> as I.
> But if they cannot contain, let them marry:
> for it is better to marry than to burn.

(Bertrand Russell, in 1929, wisecracked about this passage: "I remember once being advised by a doctor to abandon the practice of smoking, and he said that I should find it easier if, whenever the desire came upon me, I proceeded to suck an acid drop. It is in this spirit that St. Paul recommends marriage.")

St. Paul's position on remarriage after divorce was to be much debated in the next two millennia:

> And unto the married I command, yet not
> I, but the Lord, Let not the wife depart from
> the husband:
> But and if she depart, let her remain
> unmarried, or be reconciled to her husband:
> and let not the husband put away his wife.

Then St. Augustine in the fifth century A.D. made things even more complicated by claiming that marriage was a sacred bond if it is entered into in the Church, and hence could not be dissolved in any way except by death. He used the word "sacrament," which did not yet have the rigid meaning it came to have with St. Thomas Aquinas in the thirteenth century. By then marriage had become one of the seven sacraments, a symbol of the unity of Christ and the Church, hence a holy state. All possibility of divorce was ruled out.

Meanwhile, the still-unconverted pagan peoples of northern Europe allowed divorce, primarily to the husband. About the time of Charlemagne, these northerners began to allow divorce by mutual consent. It was Charlemagne who tried, with only partial success, to turn the position of the Church into law and make all the people follow it. In the absence of any sources on either marriage or divorce in the Roman law (which was widely followed at the time), the law of the Church, canon law, was given control over everything that had to do with marriage. Canon 1012 Paragraph 1 states that

> Christ our Lord elevated the very contract
> of marriage between baptised persons to the
> dignity of a sacrament.

The belief was still held, however, that the first act of marital sexual intercourse, not the contract, created the sacramental bond. The Church provided annulment for any marriage that had not been sexually consummated, and the parties could remarry.

Canon law was something new and unique. Both Judaism and Islam combine law and religion, but in both cases the law was "swallowed up" by religion. For orthodox Jews and Muslims there is no room for political authorities—everything is from God, so that legal science coincides with theology. But Christians from the first handled it differently. They not only recognized the political authorities, but in the case of canon law, imitated them. They recognized the realm of Caesar as distinct from the realm of God, and bade us render unto each what was due to him. Centuries later people argued about whether marriage and the family properly fall into one realm or the other. The history of England and all the countries whose systems of government derived from England would be very different if that distinction had not been made.

Canon law allowed two kinds of partial dissolution: divorce *a vinculo* or "divorce from the chains," and a kind of judicial separation called divorce *a mensa et thoro*—a "divorce from bed and board," which was actually not a divorce at all, but did relieve the couple from some of the requirements of the marriage contract. In neither case could people remarry.

From the earliest times there were three "grounds" for divorce: adultery, "spiritual adultery," and cruelty. "Spiritual adultery" seems to have meant heresy, but may well have been confused with apostasy. Annulments could also be had on several other grounds. The easiest was to prove some sort of a kinship relationship that the principals claimed not to have known at the time the marriage was undertaken. Another way was called the ground of "precontract": that one of the parties was not free to make the marriage because he or she had already made another pledge. It was, of course, quite easy to say that you had exchanged mutual promises of marriage with somebody else. The parties could remarry even if the first marriage had been consummated.

The wedding ceremony held inside the church was a relatively late arrival in Christian history. Only after about 1300 did the priest come to be the official who pronounced the marriage, thereby making it "legitimate" in the sense that the children were recognized and property rights were established. But most people at that time did not bother to get married in church. It was expensive, and provided no more legal protection than did marriages by contract between husband and wife or between their families.

Thus, though there was no recognized form of

divorce in medieval Europe, husbands had little trouble in getting rid of wives and marrying others under the name of annulment. Medieval documents are full of complaints that men trade wives like horses or that people do not live up to their marriage arrangements. The documents complained that marriage was going to the dogs.

With the Council of Trent—actually a series of conferences held between 1545 and 1563—marriage was pronounced to be absolutely indissoluble because it was a sacrament. All the other aspects of marriage and family were reduced to Christian "ethics," that is, good Christians were supposed to work toward a good marriage relationship, but there were no enforceable standards for any aspects of marriage other than the sacramental one. The quality of the relationship was thus deemed all but irrelevant. However, some twentieth-century authorities see this form of marriage as improving the position of women, for it gave them status and some rights in the eyes of the Church.

With the Protestant Reformation, a great struggle between Church and State surfaced, leading ultimately to a compromise between God and Caesar. The Protestants wanted marriage in the realm of Caesar, while the traditional Roman Catholic position was that it must remain in the realm of God. Martin Luther said specifically that marriage and divorce were the business of the secular government—not matters of the Church, but "worldly things." Marriage was in his view a serious institution, but not a religious one. Unlike St. Paul, Luther regarded marriage as the estate vastly preferable to all others. He claimed that when Christ commented on the matter, he was acting as a politician and policeman, not talking about the attitudes of God.

In Luther's opinion the *law* ought to allow divorce. However, he also believed that Christians should live such lives that they need never resort to any such law. Only in cases of adultery and desertion, Luther held, should Christians divorce. Thus he retained most of the older ideas about marriage and divorce, and by insisting the good Christians would never need such a law, he laid the foundation for the idea of "failure" that centuries later was to haunt so many persons.

> One spouse may rob and withdraw himself
> or herself from the other and refuse to grant
> the conjugal due or to associate with the other.
> One may find a woman so stubborn and
> thickheaded that it means nothing to her
> though her husband fall into unchasteness ten
> times. Then it is time for the man to say: If
> you are not willing, another woman is; if the
> wife is not willing, bring on the maid. But this
> is only after the husband has told his wife
> once or twice, warned her, and let it be known
> to other people that her stubborn refusal may
> be publicly known and rebuked before the
> Congregation. If she still does not want to
> comply, then dismiss her.

Other Protestant leaders such as John Calvin and Huldreich Zwingli in Switzerland advanced similar if more cautious views.

In England, the marital troubles of King Henry VIII, which led to the breakaway of the Anglican Church from the Church of Rome, also led him to appoint a committee under Archbishop Cranmer to look into the matter of divorce. Its report, issued just after Henry's death and called the *Reformatio Legum Ecclesiasticum*, established absolute divorce on grounds of adultery, cruelty, and "such violent hatred as rendered it in the highest degree improbable that the husband and wife would survive their animosities and again love one another."

However, this modern-sounding idea held sway for only about fifty years. In 1602, during the reign of Henry's daughter, Elizabeth I, a court declared any second marriage of a person so divorced to be invalid. That decision was a victory for the Anglican conservatives and a bitter defeat for the Puritans and other dissenting Protestants, who demanded that all marriage cases should be in the hands of civil authorities. The Separatists, a radical group of Puritans, went so far as to claim that there should be no religious marriage ceremony at all, and that marriages could be dissolved by a private divorce, like a *get*. Indeed, that change in the law was one of the Puritans' many grounds for resistance to the Church of England and the crown.

Divorce was handed to the British civil courts only centuries later, in 1858, during Victoria's reign. But in that long period between Elizabeth I and Victoria, the usual way to divorce—at least for the rich and well placed—was by a special act of Parliament. This was the situation that the poet John Milton railed against in his famous defense of divorce: "The Popes of Rome . . . wrought so upon the superstition of those ages, as to divest them of (the right of divorce) which God from the beginning had entrusted to the husband. . . The absolute and final hindering of divorce cannot belong to any civil or earthly power, against the will and consent of both parties, or of the husband alone."

Milton, whose ideas sound astonishingly modern, urged that spouses "part with wise and quiet consent betimes," rather than "still to foil and profane that mystery of joy and union with a polluting sadness and perpetual distemper." It was not the sacrament or the law that made the marriage continue, he said, but the continuing "peace and love, whether in marriage or in divorce." Milton's most famous statement about marriage is a paraphrase of the Bible: "If it be unlawful for man to put asunder that which God hath joined, let man take heed it be not detestable to join that by compulsion which God hath put asunder."

Another significant legacy of the past, based on the ancient concern with grounds and on the partial divorce recognized in canon law, took a new form in the seventeenth century: the idea, in analogy to contract law, that divorce is punishment of the party guilty of marital misconduct and a reward to the innocent party. The corollary is that divorce must result from an adversary procedure. That is, the two parties to a marriage must confront one another as if they were involved in the breach of some more ordinary contract. One spouse had publicly to find fault with the way the other dealt with the contractual aspects of the relationship.

The premise that a judge had to find one party guilty of some misdeed and the other party innocent led to the idea that if *both* parties to a marriage were guilty of misconduct, no divorce could be granted. That idea hung on in the United States until 1970—any defendant's "defense" against being divorced was not only his or her own innocence, but the "marital misconduct" of the plaintiff. This defense was more commonly used by a wife to get support than to stop a divorce, but often the support could be achieved only by stopping the actual divorce, and settling for the older style of divorce from bed and board (*mensa et thoro*).

Caught in this bind, the desperate became clever. The rich hit on the idea of divorce as an act of Parliament. Apparently the first parliamentary divorce was granted by a special act in 1669. Lord Roos, who had already got a divorce from bed and board through an ecclesiastical court, requested the House of Lords to pass a bill permitting him to remarry. Parliamentary divorce remained rare, almost surely because it was so expensive. Only 5 cases seem to have occurred before 1715. There were 60 between then and 1775—1 a year. The rate increased a little, to 74 in the next 24 years; there were 90 in the years 1801–1850.

When British colonists came to the New World, they brought their ideas about marriage and divorce with them. The first wedding among the English colonists in America was the remarriage of two people who had been widowed in the severe first winter the Puritans spent at Plymouth. It was carried out by a civil authority, in keeping with the Puritans' views.

The Puritans in the Massachusetts Bay Colony followed much the same custom as the Puritans of Plymouth. Marriages were solemnized by magistrates, and it was not until 1692 that ministers were even allowed to perform wedding ceremonies. Civil divorces were recognized in the earliest surviving compilation of Massachusetts laws, that of 1660. Historians have found about 40 divorces in Massachusetts between 1639 and 1692, but the records are incomplete and there probably were more. In 1692, an act amending the Second Charter required the Governor and Council to hear all marriage and divorce action. A few years later, grounds for divorce were formalized: impotence, bigamy, adultery, incest, fornication before marriage with a relative of the spouse, malicious desertion, and presumption of death after a long absence. Although these grounds were more liberal, their source in Catholic canon law is clear. Data on Massachusetts divorces are pretty spotty until 1760, but in the years 1760–1786, for which records seem to be complete, there were 96 divorce cases. Both Connecticut and Rhode Island provided legislative divorces as well as judicial ones. The grounds were adultery, fraudulent contract, willful desertion "with total neglect of duty," and presumption of death after seven years' absence. The Connecticut law remained in effect until the end of the Colonial period.

In Virginia, where there were no Puritans, the Anglican Church held full sway and English ecclesiastical law was enforced. In other southern colonies—Maryland, the Carolinas, Georgia—civil marriage was permitted, but not encouraged. In the Middle Atlantic states, the situation varied. There is no evidence that any divorces were granted at all in New York from 1675 to the end of the Colonial period. Pennsylvania had a more liberal divorce law from early times. After 1700, divorce was decreed as *punishment* for adultery, bestiality, or bigamy. Other grounds were soon added. The General Assembly of Pennsylvania passed a bill of legislative divorce in 1769, another in 1772, which was later disallowed by the British Privy Council.

Thus, the picture varied: divorce was fully recognized in New England, absolutely forbidden in the laws of the southern colonies and New York; it occurred occasionally in Pennsylvania and New Jersey. We have had all different shades of legal opinion ever since.

After the revolution, the Constitution left matters of marriage and divorce (along with many others) to the various states. We have always had as many jurisdictions as there are states (plus one for the District of Columbia and sometimes for territories as well). It would, to this day, take an Amendment to the Constitution for the federal government to regulate marriage and divorce.

Although judicial divorce was available in most states, most also continue to pass bills of divorce through their legislatures, for the most part for people who did not fall clearly under the general statutes. Divorce did not become completely a matter for the courts until the eve of the Civil War. It was 1848 when legislative divorce was ended in Virginia, 1850 in Georgia. Delaware was apparently the last state to give up legislative divorce, in 1897.

Another important development for the divorce practices of America occurred in 1867 when Massachusetts imported the idea of the interlocutory decree from Britain. People were forbidden to remarry for six months or even a year after being granted a divorce.

Throughout the first 100 years of the republic, the divorce rate rose slowly, and from the beginning there was always an outcry over whatever it was. In 1804, for example, Timothy Dwight, a famous minister who was also president of Yale, publicly noted that in a period of five years, 400 divorces had been granted in Connecticut, one for every 100 married couples. "What a flaming proof is here of the baleful influence of this corruption on a people, otherwise remarkably distinguished for their intelligence, morals, and religion!"

The rising divorce rate continued to attract attention.

Nelson Blake, in his 1962 book The Road to Reno, which is still the best general history of divorce in America, cites the Cleveland Herald's rude comments on the Ohio Supreme Court's hearing over 200 divorce cases in 1833 in addition to 50 applicants for legislative divorce. A few years later, the Cincinnati Herald praised the Ohio legislature for refusing to pass divorce bills in 1846, and for sending all divorce action to the courts.

In general, frontier states tended to be liberal. Divorce was more readily obtainable in the northwestern states and territories than in the East.

Another event that vastly affected American divorce practice was migration to the West in the 1800s. Some settlers didn't bother to get divorced before they remarried. Courts soon assumed that any current marriage was valid. If matters concerning earlier marriages came to court, the court favored the present wife over the previous one. The legacy of this presumption is with us to this day; social surveys show that public opinion favors the second wife over the first wife, and even over the first wife's children.

After the Civil War, the issue of women's rights fully emerged. Women leaders saw divorce as a central issue, but could not agree on what should be done. Women began to claim that as the victims of marriage, they should have the right to divorce, reviving a point at least as old as the Greeks—that divorce was less an evil than the sufferings created by an unhappy marriage.

Amelia Bloomer said that every woman with children who was married to a drunkard should be required to get a divorce. One of Elizabeth Cady Stanton's most impassioned statements still rings: "It is vain to look for the elevation of woman so long as she is degraded in marriage. I say it is a sin, an outrage on our liberal feelings to pretend that anything but deep fervent love and sympathy constitute marriage."

Stanton spent her life trying to get people to recognize that marriage based on the quality of personal relationships is to be preferred to marriage based on traditional religious or legal concepts. She and her colleagues were interested in the wife's right to her own body and her own property. As early as the annual women's rights convention in 1860, Stanton offered ten resolutions, based more or less on Milton. As Blake describes it, Stanton's opinion was that "the trouble with marriage . . . was that the male sex had had the sole regulation of the matter." Some feminists, like Mrs. Oakes Smith, took an opposite position: "People marry at their peril at best; let them abide by the consequences." They claimed that if a husband went bad, the wife should patiently and lovingly use all her influence to bring him back to the proper path. This difference of opinion could still be found in the 1960s and 1970s, the women's movement echoing Stanton, organizations like Fascinating Womanhood echoing Smith.

People could not grasp during the final third of the nineteenth century that the family was undergoing a profound change, not so much in structure as in its social context. As Elaine Tyler May discovered by close examination of divorce cases in Los Angeles and New Jersey in 1880 and in 1920, people continued to mouth Victorian platitudes while their actions were changing significantly. As men turned more and more to industrial jobs, they created romantic paeans about the place of women in the home. The women were convinced— May's cases document this point clearly—that they needed protecting even as more and more of them entered the labor market. A loose society, in which the community was primary, had given way to what historian William L. O'Neill has called a "tightly segmented social order divided into classes that are further subdivided into conjugal families." These changes made society's demands on the family more abstract—the family was told to rear "good" children rather than merely teach them what to do. The idea emerged that families are both the centerpiece of the increasingly complex society and a surcease from its cruel demands. The ideas of happiness in marriage were also changing. May, in *Great Expectations: Marriage and Divorce in Post-Victorian America*, shows clearly that an ethic of obligation was giving way to an ethic of gratification at the very time that the idea about what makes a person a good spouse was becoming ever more personalized.

This new context pushed family members closer and closer together. Once people could skirt the family, living the most important parts of their lives away from home, but now there was no way out. If that kind of family was to work, divorce was essential to those who could not manage the new closeness and the new systems of power.

These ideas of equitable marriage got mixed up with another topic that seemed no more daring at that time: free love. Stanton was widely attacked about, and some of her associates such as Victoria Woodhull were deeply involved in, the free love movement. But Stanton's position was straightforward: "The wisest possible reform we could have on this whole question is to have no legislation whatever. The relations of the sexes are too delicate in their nature for statutes, lawyers, judges, jurors, or our public journals to take cognizance of or regulate."

We can see today that people in those days still confused the tragedy (or sometimes melodrama) of marital breakdown with the institution of divorce. Alarmed by, and attempting to stop, change in the family, they had it backward: divorce cannot *cause* marital breakdown. The problem was not in the law, but in changing social and economic conditions. People did not see—as many still do not see—that a high divorce rate does *not* have to mean an unstable family.

It can even be argued that the family became *more* stable during the period of rising divorce, for the simple reason that the death rate was dropping throughout the second half of the nineteenth century. In fact, more families were staying together longer because people were living longer. The combined rate of marital termination by death and divorce was 33 per thousand marriages in the 1860s, but only 27 per thousand marriages in the 1950s. Not until about 1970 had the death rate stabilized to the point that the expanding divorce rate began to catch up to it. However, death, unlike divorce, does not seem immoral.

All the while, another kind of change was taking place. People were leaving their homes and going to other states where they could get easier or quicker divorces. Adultery was the sole ground for divorce in New York until 1967; South Carolina repealed all its divorce laws in 1878, and no more divorces were granted in that state until 1949. At least as early as 1787, just after the founding of the republic, New Yorkers were establishing residence in other states, getting divorces, then returning to New York. Pennsylvania was one of the earliest divorce havens for distressed New Yorkers. About 1840, the trade moved west to Ohio, Indiana, and Illinois. After the Civil War, Chicago became the center of migratory divorce. Ads appeared in eastern papers for divorce mills in others states. As many as a quarter of the divorce decrees in Illinois and Indiana and perhaps a sixth in Connecticut were apparently arranged by lawyers in New York, with only an agent or accomplice filing papers in the state where the divorce was actually granted. The divorce industry was born.

Utah, in the 1850s, defined a resident as anyone who lived in Utah or wished to live there. Thus Utah divorce laws applied everywhere, and business boomed until the traditionalists got the upper hand. Then "intent" no longer sufficed and residence requirements were extended to a year. Indiana tightened up its residence laws in 1873 from one to two years, because much of the population felt besmirched by the state's divorce activities.

By the 1870s and 1880s, migratory divorce centered in Rhode Island, Iowa, and the District of Columbia.

Then, when the Dakotas were admitted to the union in 1889, they kept the Dakota Territory's earlier three-month residence requirement. Sioux Falls became the center of American migratory divorce. But here again, crusading conservative forces succeeded in extending the period for residence.

In the 1890s, Oklahoma lawyers sent out circulars advertising divorce services and detailing the steps to a quick, cheap divorce. Wyoming also had its turn in the late 1890s. But the shift from opportunism to conservatism was the rule after 1908, by which time only Texas, Nebraska, Idaho, and Nevada had six-month residence requirements.

By the 1920s Nevadans knew they depended on tourists for their prosperity. Open and legally controlled gambling had not yet caught on, although plenty of gambling was probably taking place. Nevada legislators knew that one of the best ways to get those tourist dollars was to retain liberal divorce laws. Despite campaigns by conservatives and the clergy, in 1927 the residence requirement was reduced: you could get a divorce by living in Nevada for three months.

The struggle heated up. By 1931 Arkansas and Idaho had also reduced their residence requirements to three months. In response, Nevada reduced its residence requirements to six weeks and offered an added attraction. All divorce cases would be tried in the judge's chambers, and the records sealed, so that nobody need ever know the grounds.

The ploy was so successful that Nevadans began to worry that their economy would collapse if New York ever changed its divorce laws. From about 1,000 divorces in 1920, the number jumped to 2,500 by 1928. After the residence requirement was changed to six weeks in 1931, it climbed to 5,260; in 1943 it rose to 11,000, and to 20,500 in 1946. During the 1950s, when the divorce rate temporarily slowed, it settled in at about 10,000.

Nevada had foreign as well as domestic competition

for the divorce trade. France offered easy divorces to Americans, and so did nearby Mexico. Ciudad Juarez, in the state of Chihuahua, across the river from El Paso, Texas, became a divorce capital in the years after the Mexican Revolution of 1914. Although Mexico had not previously allowed divorce at all, the new laws allowed divorce for "valid causes" including mutual consent. The new law was intended for the poor, who chose illegitimate unions rather than divorce and remarriage, but North Americans pounced on it. Establishing residence amounted to signing a book at the City Hall and paying 150 pesos. The parties could then notify the registrar that they agreed to terminate the marriage, and it was done. Indeed, under Chihuahua law, attorneys could appear for the principals, who didn't have to make the trip to El Paso. You could even get a mail order divorce from Mexico. Historian Nelson Blake found in a 1935 issue of the New York *Daily Mirror* an advertisement placed by American attorneys in Mexican law offices, specializing in divorces. The standard fee was $225.

In 1939, the Virgin Islands decided to add to its other tourist attractions and reduced its residence requirements for divorce to six weeks. In the late 1940s and the 1950s, Alabama began to grant divorces if either of the parties was subject to Alabama law. To be subject to Alabama law, you got a lawyer to tell the court that you had just come to Alabama and intended to stay for the required year.

The rise of migratory divorce in the late nineteenth and early twentieth centuries strained the section of the Constitution that provides that every state give full faith and credit to the judicial proceedings of every other state. In 1873, the Supreme Court interpreted this to mean that the statute applied *only* if the state in which the trial occurred had jurisdiction, reducing a migratory divorce case to a fight about whether or not the state that gave the divorce actually had jurisdiction. Some states claimed that short periods of residence did not in fact create the jurisdiction, particularly when the new "resident" left that state immediately after divorce.

The Supreme Court finally settled this matter in 1949 by deciding that if the litigants actually appeared at the divorce hearing, and if the state in which it occurred claimed to have jurisdiction, then the other states had to give faith and credit. However, a lot of loose ends remained. The Court said that if both parties did not appear at their own hearings, the "incidental rights arising out the marriage" might be questioned in another state, even if the divorce itself had been made strictly legal by appearance of a proxy or an attorney. The Court, in 1957, upheld a New York decision to which the State of New York awarded a wife a support order after her husband got a Nevada divorce. To this day it is possible to get contradictory custody orders in two states.

Pressure for uniform laws focused on attempts to get all the states to adopt uniform laws and on attempts to amend the Constitution. The first meeting of an organization called the National Conference of Commissioners on Uniform State Laws was held in Saratoga, New York, in 1892. By the early 1970s, this body, composed of appointed representatives of each state, had drafted 185 model laws, but the only one to show much success was the Uniform Commercial Code, which was adopted by all but one state. Though the Commission had originally been organized to deal with the problem of migratory divorce, it had to wait for more than fifty years, until 1947, for its first success in matrimonial law, when one of their statutes was actually adopted by nine states. However, by 1980, the Commission's statute on "no-fault" divorce, following closely the California law of 1969, had affected the new laws of all but two states.

A motion to amend the Constitution in hope of regulating marriage and divorce was introduced in every Congress from 1884 to 1949. When Franklin Roosevelt was a New York state senator in 1911, he proposed that the New York legislature back a Constitutional amendment to establish a uniform law of marriage and divorce throughout the country. In 1923 Senator Capper of Kansas introduced a Constitutional amendment. Introduced every year until 1949, it never passed. Such groups as the Association for the Sanctity of Marriage, fearing that the federal laws would have to be more liberal than the laws of some states, lobbied against them. On the other hand, many liberals worried that federal laws would be stricter than the laws of their states, a step backward for what they thought of as the rationalization of divorce.

In spite of all the outcry, divorce *laws* were no more liberal in the middle of the twentieth century than they had been a hundred years earlier. Until 1970, the laws did not change much, but practice changed as the divorce rate inexorably rose. A fundamental shift in attitude was taking place, expressed in the words of a Florida authority in the mid-1940s: "Our courts in Florida . . . have in recent years, through their decisions in matrimonial matters, gotten away from the question of personal or intentional guilt. Florida more and more is treating the question of marriage relations and divorce from not only the external facts, but the internal psychology of the individuals involved."

Throughout this period, marriage was coming to be considered as a rewarding psychological union. Americans emphasized not the right to get married, but the right to a "happy" marriage. By the 1930s, even the courts began to admit that when people could not get out of marriages, the result was (in the words of an opinion handed down from the U.S. Court of Appeals) "perjury, bigamy and bastardy" as well as unhappiness. When the Charleston, South Carolina, League of Women Voters got behind an attempt to reintroduce divorce law into their state, they argued that "when a married couple no longer accepted their mutual agreement, no amount of legal force could keep them married." It sounds astonishingly like Milton.

Pleas for a recognition of marriage as a contract solely between the parties, and for psychotherapy as a mode of dealing with marital problems, appeared. In 1948, Reginald Heber Smith, a Boston lawyer and one of the organizers of Legal Aid, put these ideas forward at the White House Conference on the Family, and soon thereafter an Interprofessional Commission on Marriage and Divorce Laws was set up under the headship of Judge Paul Alexander of Toledo, Ohio, one of the leaders of divorce reform. The report of the White House conference advanced arguments that in the next thirty years were to become standard: divorce based on guilt and punishment destroys family stability; adversary procedures in divorce cases are counterproductive; the therapeutic approach in a family court would work best.

Under Alexander's leadership, the idea of the family court quickly caught on. There had been experiments in Cincinnati as early as 1914, and by 1938 the Ohio legislature had allowed Ohio divorce courts to investigate the family relations, conduct, and finances of the parties to the divorce. By 1951, such examinations were required, and professional staffs were being hired. Family courts soon appeared in Milwaukee, St. Louis, Omaha, Portland, Oregon, and Washington, D.C., which began to take the attitudes and needs of children into consideration.

Another turning point came in 1952. The California Supreme Court, when it heard an appeal on *DeBurgh vs. DeBurgh*, questioned the old idea that divorce could be granted only if an innocent party could prove marital fault. In that case, Mrs. DeBurgh brought a case against her husband on grounds of extreme cruelty. He filed a countersuit on the same grounds. The lower court applied the law as it literally was written: neither of the DeBurghs was entitled to a divorce because there was fault on both sides. No divorce was granted.

The silliness of such a doctrine was glaringly apparent. Evidence at the trial indicated that on many occasions the husband had inflicted "severe bodily injury" on his wife. On one occasion, the wife attempted suicide by swallowing sleeping pills. It was shown that he often boasted to company in her presence about his sexual exploits. On the other hand, he showed that she had written to his business partner calling him dishonest and homosexual and threatened to write such letters to everybody else he did business with. A law that forced these two people to stay married because there was no "innocent party" seemed absurd.

Justice Traynor of the California Supreme Court reversed the decision of the lower court in an opinion ringing with the new ideology: "The deceptive analogy to contract law ignores the basic fact that marriage is a great deal more than a contract. It can be terminated only with the consent of the state. Since the family is the core of our society, the law seeks to foster and preserve marriage. But when a marriage has failed and the family has ceased to be a unit, the purposes of family life are no longer served and divorce will be permitted. Public policy does not discourage divorce where the relations between husband and wife are such that the legitimate objects of matrimony have been utterly destroyed."

Then in 1960, sociologist Ivan Nye of the State College of Washington dropped a bombshell. His research indicated that "the children of divorced parents suffered less from psychological ailments, were less inclined toward delinquency and had better relationships with their parents than children whose parents quarrelled perpetually." Nye's findings were welcome, and widely accepted, without very much corroborating research on other samples. People seemed just to "know" it was right, that is, it was what they wanted to hear. Today criticisms of Nye's research are beginning to come in, and some psychotherapists no longer subscribe to this idea unconditionally, but his idea remains influential.

A watershed was finally reached in 1969 when the California legislature altered the law of divorce in that state. The statute can kindly be called jerry-built, for in spite of all the planning, it was hastily put together from several sources. The law contains some contradictions and several undefined terms. Nevertheless, this law, together with the statute that the Commission on Uniform State Laws based on it, were adopted as models in most jurisdictions in the country within a few years.

The 1969 California law does not use the word "divorce." Under it, marriages can be "dissolved." The difference seemed important at the time because the word divorce was associated with an adversary process, and the intention of the new law was to limit such action when marriages collapsed. The point of the new law was to remove all reference to "fault" in the divorce process. Underlying that idea was the belief that marriage is an ongoing relationship rather than merely a state recognized by law or by a congregation. In the 1960s it was said that "it takes two to tango." That meant that the fault could probably never be all on one side. And most people could cite successful marriages despite grievous fault by one partner. Fault concerns only one party's "faultering"; a relationship concerns two. The California law stipulates that evidence concerning the "fault" or "cause" of the breakdown of the marriage is not admissible into court.

Under the California law, "fault" is admissable in only two situations. It can be introduced into a contested case to prove irreconcilable differences. Far more important is that fault as a parent (not as a spouse) can be introduced when custody of children is in dispute. It has become evident only since the change of the law that a few people want to fight in court, because branding the other partner guilty gives them some satisfaction and may make their adjustment to divorce easier. As a result, although the number of custody cases is far smaller than it used to be, those that actually are heard are more bitterly fought.

California already had another law that makes the judge's job easier at the time of divorce: it is one of nine "community property" jurisdictions in the country (the others are Arizona, Idaho, Louisiana, Montana, New Mexico, Puerto Rico, Texas, and Washington). This law provides that everything that is owned by the spouses individually at the time of the marriage and anything that either inherits during the time of the marriage is "separate property." Everything, including wages, acquired during the marriage is "community property" and half belongs to each partner. In California, there is never much room for argument about who gets what. If the matter goes to court, the judge will tell them to sell everything and split the proceeds. These matters are usually settled out of court.

It is estimated that between a quarter and a half of the marital dissolutions in California in 1981 were awarded without the assistance of any lawyers at all. If there are no property disputes and no children, there need be no judicial hearing. Advised by the several guidebooks now on the market, the couple fill out their own papers and have them approved and filed. After a waiting period of six months, they are free to remarry.

Some feminists pointed out that the "tenure" of housewives was dealt a serious blow by the no-fault laws. Raina Eisler states that women who made home-making a career suddenly lost a lot: "As more and more women become unemployed as wives . . . they are forced to find other jobs. . . . An ever-growing number of these divorced women or 'unemployed' housewives cannot and will not be absorbed into the general economy. . . . The only recourse has been to join the nation's poor." She goes on to say that the new divorce laws are based on different premises from the marriage laws (which is true in most societies).

What some critics consider the greatest difficulty of all has appeared in states that do not recognize community property. In the "common law" property states, at the time of divorce it becomes necessary to determine what is "marital property," which then must be divided "equably." The law is based on an analogy to dissolution of a business partnership. A woman in a common-law state has no rights to any marital property except what the court awards her; everything that is not in her name is considered to belong to the husband. The law for dividing marital property differs widely among states. In the early 1980s, both feminists and matrimonial attorneys claimed that the issue of "equitable distribution" was the most intractable one they faced.

It has also been shown that child support payments rarely provide even half of the money required to bring up a child. And study after study shows that from 40 to 79 percent of fathers are paying nothing at all. Stricter enforcement began with mothers on welfare, and spread. At first women could demand that support payments be deducted from their children's fathers' wages. The federal government soon followed, agreeing to garnishee wages of all federal employees for the purpose of paying child support. Congress also set up a federal service to locate delinquent parents, which worries civil libertarians because it is the first approved use of all military, social security, and Internal Revenue Service records to track down individuals.

But even the people who object to the new law of "dissolution" admit that it has cut down vastly on the bitterness of the legal proceedings. Many are convinced, however, that no-fault itself is a patch job, and that a complete remodeling of marriage law is still essential.

Although some people remain unalterably opposed to divorce, most others are thinking more creatively about marriage—and especially about the family—than ever before. Perhaps most important, we are finally able to dissociate the facts of miserable marriage as a problem from the facts of divorce as a solution. Our ideas about marriage and divorce have finally shaken off the shackles of ancient tradition—although people of the twenty-first century will probably say the same about theirs.

3

Other Kinds of Marriages

Whenever the family changes a little, Americans shudder, usually publicly, and declaim that the family is breaking down. A people more sophisticated in family forms would know it isn't so.

Because Americans lack broad experience in family matters, they have trouble seeing as valid any families except the kind they grew up in. Yet there are many ways to validate a marriage, just as there are many ways to get divorced, some of them more and some less miserable than our own. There are many ways to bring up children, and just as many ideas about where children come from, what you have to do or avoid to get them or not get them.

In many societies of the world, a man is allowed or encouraged to have more than one wife at a time, which amounts to having several simple families at once. In this way, he can have far more legitimate children than any one wife could provide. In societies where wealth and status, and perhaps immortality, depend on having children, polygyny is highly regarded—always by men, and usually by women.

In order to understand what our families are, it is a good idea to look at some of the things they are not. On the same principle that you can understand your native language more fully if you know another, I propose that you can't really understand monogamy fully until you understand polygyny. And to understand polygyny, you

64

must first put your way of thinking about marriage to one side. I do not say you have to give up your values or change your habits, but you ought to know that they are your chosen values and not eternal verities. The first thing we have to do when we think about other kinds of families is to move the relationship between the spouses out of central position. What goes on in a marriage is different in polygynous society from what it is in monogamous society. When there are two wives, marriage becomes far more a role relationship and far less a personal relationship. Attention goes to the parental relationships.

A polygynous society must provide answers to questions that don't come up in a monogamous society. What is the relationship among co-wives? What is the relationship among groups of half-siblings? In our society, half-siblings are almost always different ages, but in polygynous societies they are not. And, perhaps most telling of all, what kind of relationship can exist between a man and a wife when there is more than one wife?

Many years ago, when I was studying the Tiv in Nigeria, my cook asked me for an advance of 10 pounds on his salary. That was a lot of money, almost twice his monthly pay. I asked what he wanted it for. He said that he was tired of begetting other people's children and that he was going to use it for bridewealth (anthropological jargon for the sum he would pay his bride's parents in return for accepting him as her husband and releasing some rights to her children to him and his people). I made him the advance, and he brought home his bride.

What we both knew, but did not consider worth mentioning, is that he already had a wife who was living on his farms "at home" with her (and his) three children. The youngest of those children was only a little over a year old. Tiv women remain celibate during the entire period that they are nursing babies—up to three years. They do not expect their husbands to do the same. Therefore, they tell me, it is sensible for him to take a new wife while he is away doing his job and she stays home tending her children and her farm. She could devote herself fully to the well-being of her children, could provide all her own food, and get help with the children from his brothers' wives. Americans, who have good medical services to help them assure their children's health, as she did not, see her action as an example of low status of women. In fact, it reveals the low status of medical achievement.

Our main example in this chapter will be the Mormon experience with polygyny in the United States in the nineteenth century—an interesting experiment, although social pressures on the Mormons made it difficult to establish the system in its entirety, and even harder to maintain it through several generations. We will then look briefly at polyandry in India and Tibet.

The Mormon experiment with polgyny illustrates vividly both the way polygynous living differs from monogamous, and the way in which the male drive to paternity—not the sex drive—underlies any system of plural wives. Sex is, in almost all societies, available outside marriage. Paternity usually is not.

The Mormon Church was organized in 1830 by Joseph Smith, who claimed that the Christian Church, as established by Christ, did not survive, but that revelations from God allowed him to reestablish the true church. He gathered followers near his upper New York State home; soon after, his neighbors began to gossip, saying that Joseph Smith was thoroughly immoral because he espoused a doctrine of many wives. Fawn Brody said in her biography of Smith that "he could not rest until he had redefined the nature of sin."

Mormon polygyny made sense in terms of what Mormons called the doctrine of eternal progression, one of the cornerstones of their theology. It teaches that God was once human, that He progressed through many transformations to become God, and that other men can follow in His footsteps. Ultimately they too can become gods, each with his own universe. Besides God the Father, this doctrine continued, there are other gods, and the head god is named Eloheim. When a Latter Day Saint married a wife or wives under the "celestial marriage system for time and eternity," he was in fact advancing in godhood. The more children he had, the better, and the faster his kingdom would grow toward his becoming a god in his own right. Since women in eternity shared the positions of their earthly husbands, it was in every woman's interest to advance her husband's interests.

The idea of eternal progression posits three "estates," the first of which can be called man's preexistence. The premise is that the spirits were created by God before bodies were created, and that the heavens are populated with unrealized spirits. The second estate is an earthly or carnal stage. The spirits, once they got human bodies, could fulfill their destiny. Some of these embodied spirits turned out to be superior to others. In the best Protestant tradition, this superiority was manifested in worldly success. The most virtuous and successful proceeded to heaven for what is called "the second resurrection." Kimball Young, an apostate Mormon sociologist who wrote and worked from the 1940s to the 1960s, called this stage "the combination of the spirit and the specially processed body that would survive forever."

There are, Young noted, three kinds of marriage among the Mormons. The first is ordinary marriage, as it was practiced by everybody else. The Mormons called this marriage "for time," because it perished with the death of one of the partners. Mormons also recognized "marriage for time and eternity," in which the pair are bound not only until death, but would remain spouses in the hereafter. The third type arose because it was also possible to marry for eternity only. This could be done by widows who had been married to their husbands only in time, or for men who had died before they had any or enough children. A man in the hereafter could, thus, have many wives, provided by his concerned survivors. Spinsters could be married in eternity to good Mormons, giving them a full and enviable position in heaven they could acquire no other way.

This can lead to a situation in which a woman may be married to one man in time and to another in eternity. Her children acknowledge their genitor on earth, but in eternity they are the children of their mother's husband-in-eternity.

Mormons today are not much concerned about divorce among people who are married for time only— such a union would be broken at death in any case. They neither condone it nor much condemn it. Divorce from marriage in eternity, however, is difficult and fairly rare. Yet, being sensible people, Mormons realize that a mismatched couple spending eternity together might be the definition of hell. Divorce from a marriage in eternity is possible only after much investigation and many attempts to get husband and wife to reconcile and live happily as Christian spouses. When that cannot be achieved, the spiritual divorce to cancel the marriage in eternity is performed ritually within the tabernacle, while the marriage in time is canceled by the legal means used by all Americans.

By extension, these practices mean that there are two kinds of spirits in heaven: those who have been married for time and eternity, and those who have been married only for time or not at all. Husbands of the first sort can go on with their ascendancy to become gods. Those who were married only for time could not become gods, but only "angels" to minister to the superior spirits.

The critics were obviously right that Mormonism was male-oriented. A woman's salvation depended on her husband and his priestly qualities and function. To be married to a man who "held the divine keys for admission to Heaven" was a woman's assurance of heaven, which she could get no other way. Many of these ideas were backed up by a literal reading of the Old Testament: Abraham had more than one wife; indeed, he also had several concubines. (The Mormons never recognized concubines, in spite of the fact that non-Mormon Americans looked at all Mormon wives except first wives as concubines.)

Although polygyny was secretly practiced earlier, it was not practiced publicly or as a matter of principle until a revelation of Divine order on August 29, 1852, claimed that polygyny was a sacred command by God to righteous Mormons. After that, polygyny was the preferred state, but obviously all Mormons could not attain it. In all known polygynous societies, there are more monogamous men at any one time than there are polygynists—it is a matter of simple demographics. Polygyny became another mark of worldly success.

To understand Mormon polygyny on its own terms instead of in the more limited terms of our common experiences, we have to remember several things. Polygyny does *not* increase the total number of children. The total number of children depends on the number of women, their values and options, and ultimately on their childbearing decisions. But polygyny does change the paternity of those children because more of the children are begotten by, or assigned legally as children of, fewer men. Therefore, when eternal salvation for women is connected with the religious qualifications of their husbands, and when eternity for men is connected with paternity, the stronger, more dominant men have more offspring than their more ordinary fellows. All children were legitimate according to Mormon belief, but not according to American law. Love was supposed to be the basic principle of all Mormon households. But this noble love was not to be confused with romantic love and certainly not with mere lust; rather it was "pure" love that could be supplemented by sexual conjugal love. The claim was made by Mormon theologians that you can love more than one wife equally in the same way that you can love more than one child equally.

Kimball Young made an intensive study of the

records of plural marriages among the Mormons and found that over half of them—53 percent—could be classified as highly successful or reasonably successful according to criteria he derived from the writings of the people themselves. About a quarter were in what he called a "moderate" position, while a little under a quarter showed considerable or severe conflict. Young also discovered that over half the polygynous families were to be found among the comfortable and well-to-do. Only one-sixth could be considered poor. As a matter of fact, polygynous societies everywhere show the same characteristic: the well-to-do are polygynous, in part because polygyny redistributes wealth less even-handedly than some other forms of family.

Here is the story of one Mormon family. Brother Hans Olson and his new wife Emma were converted to Mormonism in Sweden in 1851 and arrived in Utah in the summer of 1853. The Church first sent Olson, a millwright, to Ogden to operate a mill, then later to Logan to establish two new mills.

Polygyny was officially promulgated the year the Olsons arrived in Utah. During the next eight years, Olson married three additional wives. The first, Josephine, was a widow, already married in eternity to her first husband. The second and third, Marie and Annie, were both married to Olson for time and eternity, as was Emma. The four wives produced a total of 32 children by Olson—24 were his own in eternity; the other 8 belonged to Josephine's first husband. During the first years, the entire family lived in an adobe house in which each woman had a large room. As Olson prospered, he built a separate house for each wife; eventually he bought a farm and took one of them there. Olson's wives got along well together. Any problems were solved within the house and never fought out in the open.

Babies were, of course, under the care of their mothers. As they began to get older, the discipline of the father became more evident. Olson was a stern father, but he got along well with his children. The children like all Mormon children, called their mother's co-wives "aunt." Discipline is a touchy point in any polygynous family. In some, a woman must never discipline her co-wives' children. But in the Olson family aunts could discipline the children without making the children's mothers angry—one of the most important marks of a successful polygynous family anywhere. When Olson's fourth wife died leaving an infant, that child was brought up by the first wife, another sign of the good relations among all the wives.

Olson was well educated for the time, and he valued education for his children. So every morning he got the children up at 4 o'clock and held classes. Only later were there any adequate schools.

As Olson got older, he settled in more and more with the first wife, Emma. This pattern is often found among many polygynists. A man chooses one wife for companionship and close intimacy, not necessarily the first, but he does not turn against the others. Olson continued to treat all his wives "equally." Whenever he bought anything for one, he bought something similar for the others. When Olson died, the family took only about two hours to divide the estate amicably. It is a story of the ideal polygynous family.

In short, a successful polygynist needs administrative cunning and executive talent. The "permission" of the first wife and perhaps the others is essential before a man marries the next, else she is likely to be troublesome. Like polygynists everywhere, some Mormon men actually got that permission, but many didn't. The Church does not appear to have provided a clear model of a way for a man to handle this matter.

Occasionally first wives left when a second was brought in. One such family was that of Andrew Pope. He and his first wife were converted in England and came to Utah in the 1880s. The Popes were married in eternity, in addition to the marriage for time they had contracted in England. Mrs. Pope, however, never became a devout Mormon. Therefore, when Pope took a second wife in 1887, she picked up and left.

A few years later, the second Mrs. Pope also felt resentful when he married his third wife. The two women had little in common (a mistake for any polygynist to make). But the second had been brought up as a Mormon and believed in "the principle," as polygyny was called. She struggled, sacrificed, and won her salvation.

Before the adoption of polygyny, the Mormons were as much against divorce as were the Catholics. But polygyny, when it was first introduced, brought new pressures. In September, 1856, Brigham Young gave women two weeks to leave their marriages if they wanted to. He told the men to say to their wives, "Take all that I have and be set at liberty, but if you stay with me you shall comply with the law of God [that is, the principle of polygyny], and that too without murmuring and whining."

It is instructive that people use the same reasons to explain difficulty in polygynous marriages as they do in monogamous ones. Each culture supplies reasons why marriages turn bad, which are hauled out whatever may happen in a marriage. Among the most important reasons cited by Americans, including Mormons, are differences in age and in temperament. In addition to age differences between husbands and wives, co-wives might be of widely varying ages.

The Mormons obviously knew, but never openly acknowledged, that the secret of running any polygynous household is in the relationship among the women. The stories of successful polygynous families always indicate that that problem was solved. One man recalled: "Father was a wise man. He chose well. All three of his wives had the same ideas—they wanted education and culture, and they wanted a peaceful home."

The three of them got along together because "they knew they had to consider each other's rights."

However, the Mormons seem never to have had explicit criteria by which a co-wife could be considered successful, whether the other co-wives matched her performance or not. African polygynists always make that principle overt, but the Mormons did not move beyond the American penchant for leaving this matter to the individual.

However, difficulties in the co-wife relationship show up in many of the family histories. As one woman put it, "it is not jealousy so much, for I made up my mind for that, but the constant pressure of adjusting yourself to another woman. Each woman should be a queen in her own home, my mother always said, and it's the natural way." Some Mormon men whose wives were enemies simply withdrew in order to avoid the matter. The real problem was that the culture had not yet developed an adequate basis for handling such disputes, just as the rest of American culture has yet to find adequate ways to handle all the ramifications of divorce.

Many polygynous societies favor a man's marrying two or more sisters, because their bond as sisters may help overcome the jealousy and competition of co-wives. Other societies just as adamantly claim that the bond of sisters should not be contaminated by that of co-wives. The Mormons favored sister marriage, and it often occurred. Although it was impossible for Kimball Young to determine the exact proportion, it was evident to him that many men did marry sisters or half-sisters, and that the wives often appreciated this, sometimes going so far as to initiate the second marriage because they needed trustworthy and congenial helpmeets.

Mormon husbands alternated their time among their wives. In Young's historical sample, more than a quarter changed every day. About the same number went from one wife to another each week, while another quarter moved irregularly. The rest adjusted in their own rhythms: 2-day, 3-day, or 14-day cycles were found. The rotation was usually more frequent if all lived in the same house or close together. As is usually the case in polygynous societies, husbands neglected wives who behaved coolly toward them, and some, in spite of community disapproval stayed with favorites rather longer than pure equality of treatment would have suggested.

There was often considerable struggle for status among the wives. In the later years of the century, when government surveillance and raids against polygynists became common, the first wife achieved a new advantage in the competition for status—she was the "legal" wife. A first wife had some other advantages. Most Mormon officials usually entertained at the first wife's place and entertaining dignitaries was a symbol of status.

Being a better housekeeper, gardener, and manager was one way a co-wife could get more attention from her husband, and hence more status. Kurt Sturm's two wives, Clara and Mabel, did their level best to outwork one another. Clara was the "outside" wife who accompanied her husband. Mabel, who seems to have been physically weaker and could never keep up with Clara, was always sad that she never got to go with her husband, to be seen in the outside world. Mabel's children remembered this as a great injustice.

In monogamous families, displays of affection can be a woman's means for getting the husband's attention. However, any public exhibition of affection is necessarily strongly tabooed in polygynous society.

The number of children she bore was another mark of prestige for the woman. Children in polygynous families are strongly identified with their mothers, and with their mothers' kin. African polygynists often use the metaphor "one father, different mothers" to illustrate the way people who have a lot in common also have their differences. However, there is little in the literature on Mormons about the relationship of children with their mothers' kinsmen, particularly their mothers' brothers.

Some Mormon family stories illustrate the ingenious-
ness of co-wives in their jockeying for first place. Henry
Roper's first wife, Myra, demanded a dominant position
when the second wife, Elizabeth, appeared. According
to Myra, her family was socially several cuts above Elizabeth's family. During the first two years of her marriage, Elizabeth and Myra had to live in the same house.
But one afternoon when Henry and Elizabeth had gone
to a Church conference in Salt Lake City, Myra moved
Elizabeth's clothing, furniture, and other belongings
into another house three blocks away. Neither Henry nor
Elizabeth ever mentioned the matter to her. On another
occasion, Myra, who got up early in the morning to get
her chores done, was found throwing rocks up on the
roof of Elizabeth's house because Elizabeth and Henry
were staying in bed too late. Myra was annoyed when
Henry gave Elizabeth a heating stove, so when Elizabeth
was gone, Myra sent one of her sons to take it down and
bring it to Myra's house. Roper was angry about it, but
never did anything.

When all else failed, wives resorted to temper tantrums: "Benjamin Wolfe married two sisters, Christine
and Gertrude. . . . Once a large group of relatives came
up from Logan for the week-end to the farm where
Christine lived. Among them were other sisters of Christine and Gertrude. Both wives were present, and on
Sunday afternoon when everybody was ready to leave
for home, father decided to go back to town with Gertrude to spend Sunday night. This, of course, meant that
Christine would have to remain on the farm alone. This
precipitated an explosion. The second wife made a ter-
rific scene as we were about to depart. She could be
heard screaming a long time after the party left. Father
was about to turn back to stay with Christine when two
of her own sisters intervened, saying 'Don't you dare
give in to her.' This shamed him into going on into
town. . . . They explained that their sister had always
used such means to get her own way."

The story of David Osborne shows clearly the motivation of Mormon men to make their "principle" work. David married his first wife when he was 21 and she 16. He told her before marriage that he wanted to be polygamous: "All my life I had wanted to live in polygamy because I wanted a big family." Ten years after that first marriage, David married a second wife. The second marriage did not work out—it was the second wife, not the first, who ran away. David twice tried to get her back but failed.

Children in large numbers were important; they were the "earthly bearers of eternal spirits." Mormons are now, and have always been, doctrinally against birth control because as many spirits as possible should be allowed to be incarnated. If a child is fated to be incarnated and is kept from doing so by birth control, it is a sin, a sin against the cosmos.

"A big family," as David Osborne put it, was important to women too. Often when a woman could not conceive, she courted a second wife. We know of one of these second wives who bore seven children, the first two of whom were raised by the first wife. One remembers Abraham's wife, Sarah, who was barren and whose handmaiden bore children by her husband for her. One also thinks of the modern practice of hiring a woman to bear a man's child and handing it over, at birth, to his barren wife.

It was important for children to understand the principle of polygyny. It was not uncommon for older children of the first marriage, especially at puberty or later, to resent their father's taking a second wife. If younger children are in competition with their half-siblings, their mothers may be faced with difficult decisions: whose children are right, whose are to be corrected, whose children are "bad"? The children usually had far closer relationships with their mothers than with their fathers, which is common in both monogamous American families and polygynous African families. Part of that closeness between mother and children in polygynous families may stem from the fact that the man isn't around as much as he is in a monogamous household; certainly it also results from ideas about the nature of the father-child relationship.

There are some records of "aunts" spoiling children, indulging them more than their own mothers, probably because, with the aunts (as with grandparents), the indulgence did not have to be linked to punishment. As in all polygynous situations, however, wives were very careful when it came to disciplining their co-wives' children. The records that Young examined showed that the half-siblings themselves often got along better than their mothers did.

In polygynous societies, women depend more on their sons for support than they do in monogamous societies. Daisy Barclay wrote, "I have the attitude of many Mormon women in polygamy. I felt a responsibility to my family, and I developed an independence that women in monogamy never know. A woman in polygamy is compelled by her lone position to make a confidant of her children. How much more is this true when that woman is left entirely alone."

Fathers' responsibility for all their children included inheritance, a touchy matter in all polygynous societies. The Mormons dominated the territorial legislature of Utah and, after 1852, passed a number of laws to give equal rights to the children of all the wives, even though by that time polygyny was no longer legal in the state. The children of polygynous marriages could always inherit if their father made a will, except for the years 1887–1896. Nevertheless, Congress warned Utah repeatedly that under American law children of all wives except the first were illegitimate. After Utah became a state in January, 1896, and could pass laws of inheritance without Congressional approval, children born of plural marriages were legitimized and regained the right to inherit.

The greatest challenge to Mormon polygyny was having to adapt to a monogamy-based legal system. After 1887, the "legal" wife had a "dower right" of one-third of the estate, reflecting the custom that in the United States, wives inherit. The first, "legal" wife, usually got the largest part of any Mormon estate, which she might (and in a few cases did) share with the others. Many estates were, in those days, divided without recourse to the courts. Other estates were settled by the father's distribution of the property in anticipation of his death.

The biggest legal difficulty was making polygynous practice coincide with American law. There was even a problem about whether, on the death of the "legal" wife, a man could then "legally" marry the second wife. The Church thought that the brethren should do so. However, to many non-Mormons this arrangement was "wrong" just as marriage with the deceased wife's sister was "wrong" in many Christian countries for centuries. Many Mormons did not in fact "legally" marry their subsequent wives after the death of the first. To have done so would have been to admit that there was a difference in status among the wives in some way other than that recognized by an "outside" legal system. There was never any Mormon provision for inheriting widows as is described in the Book of Ruth or as it is practiced in Africa. There a son can "inherit" any wife except his own mother, which does indeed mean that she may bear him children, but even more importantly means that he assumes all responsibilities for her.

The secrecy that surrounded Mormon polygyny, except for a few years in the middle of its practice, seriously affected it. Not only was Mormon polygyny out of kilter with the "Christian ways" of the rest of the country, but it conflicted with the ways many Mormons themselves had been brought up before their conversion to Mormonism.

Guilt was a constant underpinning of much of what they did. That guilt is absent in an African situation or any other place where polygyny is truly integrated with the rest of the social system.

Opposition to polygyny began early. Just before the Civil War, Meta V. Fuller gushed in her book, *Mormon Wives*: "Repulsive as slavery appears to us, we can but deem polygamy a thing more loathsome and poisonous to social and political purity. Half-civilized states have ceased its practice as dangerous to happiness, and as outraging every instinct of the better nature within every breast; and as ages rolled away they left the institution behind as one of the relics of barbarism which marked the half-developed state of man as a social being."

After the slaves were liberated at the end of the Civil War, concerned public attention found a ready-made cause. The new "relic of barbarism" to be obliterated was Mormon polygyny. Because people of that era did not understand polygyny, they could not tolerate it; critics claimed that polygyny was the direst attack ever made on the American home. Indeed, the idea of marriage was so closely tied to "Christian monogamy" that ordinary people confused polygyny with prostitution and sin. When the Methodists met in Cincinnati in 1884, their Committee on Mormon Polygamy published a tract, which said, "Mormonism is not a religion, it is a crime. Therefore it cannot be entitled to protection and tolerance under the laws and Constitution of the United States." Ministers and Mormon apostates joined forces—and romance writers chipped in—in a vociferous attack on Mormon polygyny. The language got colorful—polygyny was the "rot" that would infect the marriage customs of the entire nation, turning us back into the "primitiveness" we had escaped only with immense virtuous effort.

Attacks against Mormonism centered around two points: the low position into which it was said to force women, and a hearty condemnation of male sexuality. Emerging feminism and nineteenth-century prudery both had a field day. The concern about women arose from the claims of Mormon theology that only men can become priests. Many religions allow only men into the priesthood, but comparatively few of them make all men priests, and then go on to claim that the only way women can reach salvation is to link up with a man and ride into eternity on his coattails. That is, women were cast as good wives of good Mormon husbands and not given any other way out. Some non-Mormons saw this doctrine as a way to keep women in an inferior and humiliating position.

The opposition of the self-appointed guardians of American morals was propagandistic and based on smear tactics. The most powerful weapon was to claim that all polygynists were sinfully prurient. The Gentiles, as Mormons called non-Mormons, insisted loudly that because (by their definition) no man could "love" several women at one time, the marital relations with the plural wives were therefore a dirty, nasty form of sex. They went on to argue that therefore the quality of polygynous marriage and family life was necessarily inferior. The Mormons themselves sometimes acknowledged that love, as it was prized among the Gentiles, did not exist in polygyny. However, they claimed purer feelings of respect, support, and friendship between husbands and wives. Polygynists everywhere say the same thing. This kind of respect is essential to polygyny, no matter where it occurs, just as the myth of romantic love is important to American monogamy.

Gentile propaganda focused hypocritically on the many ways plurally married women could be exploited for their labor. In fact, the work of women on the frontier in the nineteenth century was, by today's standards, almost unbelievably arduous for all women, not just the polygynously married. The degree to which plural wives were exploited more than monogamous wives cannot, obviously, be established. Neither do we yet know enough about the kind and amount of support that either got from husbands, kinsmen, children, and co-wives. Similarly, it is true that Mormon men had conrol of all property, but that had nothing to do with polygyny. It was the law and custom of the nineteenth century, and monogamous women suffered from it just as much as did their polygynously married sisters. And the Utah Gentiles' hostility was compounded by the fact that they were competing with the Mormons in politics and business.

From the middle 1880s on, the government's pressure on polygynists increased greatly. There were even attempts to disenfranchise the Mormons in Utah. As a result, many polygynists went into hiding, fleeing into remote areas of Utah, Idaho, and Arizona, and into Mexico. In 1887, almost 200 Mormons were sent to prison for polygyny, and at the end of the 1880s, Congress was told by Mormons that the Church no longer gave official permission to have more than one wife. In September, 1890, the President of the Mormon Church issued what has come to be known as the "Manifesto," announcing that the Church was no longer teaching polygamy and was forbidding its members to enter into it.

Polygyny was eventually made illegal in Utah as part of the price for persuading Congress that Utah was ready to become a state. The polygyny issue kept many in Congress from accepting Utah into the union, and the debate about Utah's statehood might have dragged on for decades had the Mormon hierarchy not given in on the issue.

Still, polygyny survived in the Mormon colonies in Mexico and in several isolated sections of the Southwest. The Mormons cleared their consciences in this matter by asserting that the Manifesto had to do with temporal law but nothing to do with the divine law. An "underground" developed to permit Mormon polygynists to hide out from the law. There are examples of second wives hiding for more than ten years. While some were sent back to their own parents, others went under assumed names to places like Franklin, Idaho, where they remained with nobody asking any questions. Sometimes the children of these women in hiding were brought up by aunts who were not in hiding. Mormon archives are full of stories like that of Angelina, Samuel Baxter's first wife; she drove all night with her horses to a farm where her husband was hiding with his second wife to warn them that the authorities were looking for them. Baxter and the second wife got away to Mexico.

In short, the Manifesto threw the Saints into confusion and doubt. The Mormon Church insisted that nobody who had made the commitment to plural wives was required to break these "covenants." Yet the law declared that only first marriages existed, which meant that many children were bastardized. The moral questions were pressing: should a man go on living with his plural wives? should he have more children? should he support the wives but not have more children? should he divorce them? should he desert them? People had to resolve these questions without answers from the authorities. As uncertainty reigned, the children of the secondary wives—now no longer wives—were teased in school; their new status became an overt basis for discrimination, as it had never been before.

The fact that plural marriages were still taking place after the Manifesto became evident in April, 1904, when a second Manifesto was issued stating that none of these new marriages had the sanction or consent of the Church. Still, polygyny continued among a small minority. One of the communities that clung most fiercely to polygyny was Short Creek, Arizona. Short Creek is one of the most isolated parts of the West, reached only over 425 miles of primitive road. It was settled about 1913, and grew rapidly because its remoteness permitted plural marriage without the knowledge or interference of government authorities. In the early 1940s, the government discovered that it was mailing welfare checks to several women in the area who all had the same husband. Six residents of the colony were charged with violation of the Mann Act, a federal law barring interstate commerce in prostitutes. In 1946 the Supreme Court upheld the conviction on the grounds that the law said you could not take a woman across a state line for immoral purposes, and that polygamy, in the premises of the law, was an immoral purpose. Short Creek came back into the news in 1953 when a police sweep caught 36 men and 86 women. Since Arizona has no antipolygamy law, other charges had to be brought—and it was decided that "a state of insurrection" would do. The men were jailed and a number of children placed in foster homes.

Today some Mormons have taken advantage of the more open attitudes created by the so-called sexual revolution to continue polygyny, or at least to bring it out into the open. A Mormon policeman is currently suing to reinstate polygyny in Utah. Dismissed from his job because he has three wives, he claims that governmental interference with the custom denies him freedom of religion. The *New York Times,* when it reported the story in September, 1983, quoted the head of the Apostolic United Brethren (a sect that still advocates polygyny) as estimating that 20,000 people in Utah live in polygynous families. It also quoted the lawyers who will oppose the policeman as saying that "while polygamy is accepted in some cultures, so are blood feuds, tribal warfare, the stoning of adulterers." Nothing, it would seem, has changed. The most interesting family experiment in American history has not really ended.

Polyandry—one woman married to several husbands—is not a mirror image of polygyny. There are differences between maternity and paternity. True polyandry, in which one woman is actually married to more than one man, is rare because polyandry does nothing for men. It enhances neither paternity nor sexuality. It does not make them richer on earth, and no prophet has yet come up with a theology in which polyandry will improve their lot in heaven.

Maternity is very little affected by any form of marriage. Whatever "disadvantages" may occur in other areas of their lives, women in polygyny are not disadvantaged as parents. Those women who understand the system are, when the advantages are great enough, willing to put up with any disadvantages. Paternity, on the other hand, *is* affected by marriage forms. Men's chances for socially recognized paternity are curtailed in monogamy and seriously curtailed in polyandry. Therefore in most polyandry, the co-husbands are brothers. If brothers share a wife or wives, they do not have to divide the family estate. In an area where land and resources are at a premium, their unity may become a primary consideration. Moreover, the children are close kin even if a husband did not himself beget them.

The Toda, a small tribe of dairying people in India when W.H.R. Rivers studied them in the first decade of the twentieth century, became the model for understanding polyandrous societies. The Toda had true polyandry in that a set of brothers all became husbands of one woman—in contrast to other groups in the area, in which the woman marries only one brother although all may have sexual access to her. Rivers found that co-husbands were always brothers, but brothers need not be co-husbands.

One of the most interesting features of Toda polyandry is that social paternity of the wife's children is acquired independently of marriage. Social paternity results from a special ceremony that Rivers called "giving the bow and arrow." Children call all their mother's husbands "father" but after the ceremony, only that brother who performed the ceremony becomes the point on the genealogy from which the children descend, until the ceremony is repeated with another husband/ brother. Once the ceremony has been performed, all that woman's children "belong" to the man who performed it, even if he dies before it is performed again with another husband. The eldest brother has the right to perform this ceremony first. Usually the ceremony is not repeated until the wife's third or fourth pregnancy,

whereupon another of the brothers performs the ceremony and takes over as socially recognized father for
two or three pregnancies. Yet, as long as the group of
brothers remains together, all are "equally regarded as
fathers of the child." Rivers' informants could, in
response to his questions, name one brother as their
father, but the name they gave was usually the most
prominent of the brothers, which means that they were
giving the name of the brother most readily identifiable.

Polyandry is conjoined with polygyny in some parts
of India and Tibet, so that a group of brothers can take
more than one wife. Rivers also found secondary forms
of marriage, in which women went to men who were not
part of the original group. However, the children they
bore still belonged to the original group.

Prince Peter of Greece and Denmark, an anthropologist who spent many years studying polyandry, went
back to the Toda and confirmed that among them all
polyandry is indeed fraternal. He was told that paternity
is usually declared by men to be important, but that
some women say it is irrelevant. Social fatherhood was
often not ascribed to an individual at all, but to the
group of brothers. The cultural emphasis is on the unity
of the brothers and on the contract between a woman
and that group of brothers.

Individual paternity may thus be culturally unim-
portant. But when there is considerable wealth to be
inherited, paternity becomes important. And when a
man's immortality is guaranteed only by the ministra-
tions of his offspring, paternity is a vital issue. Modern
sociobiology claims that paternity is important at an
unconscious level among all species, including our
own.

Polyandry among the Kota, who live nearby the Toda,
is not genuine polyandry in the sense of marriage. A
Kota woman can have only one husband and can acquire
another only after divorce or his death. However, a husband's brothers fulfill the husband's role, including his

sexual role, if he is ill, incapacitated, or otherwise unable to fulfill the duties of a husband. The household is made up of several brothers and their wives and children, in the house of their common father. When the group gets too big, the married brothers build separate houses. Kota men, besides sharing responsibilities for their wives with their brothers, may also have more than one wife, so the system includes polygyny as well as a sort of quasi-polyandry. Kota husbands are not allowed to be jealous if they find their wives sleeping with their brothers. At any sign of jealousy, the man's lineage mates bring immense pressures on him to get rid of that jealousy. However, jealousy toward any man outside this group of equivalent brothers is strongly supported. A wife's relationship with anyone who is not a husband's brother is adultery. Some anthropologists have assumed (although the evidence is not very clear) that jealousy among brothers is repressed and results in much quarreling.

Kota women are not allowed to stay alone under any circumstances. Therefore, a man who leaves for a few days asks that his brother stay in the same room with the wife to watch over her. Sometimes a man gives his wife over to his brother for some length of time, but her husband is the recognized father of all her children, whoever begets them. A man cannot question the right of his brothers to have intercourse with his wife, but paternity never goes to them. Such customs are explained by the "principle of the equivalence of brothers." That is, when it comes to representing the group, one brother will do as well as another. The brothers share alike in everything while they live in one household. Only after they split off from the household will they admit differences of status or economic prosperity. A woman does not dare to refuse her husband's brother. However, after her husband's death, she can refuse to be inherited by any of them. Once she marries someone outside that group of brothers, they no longer retain rights in her.

The same principle sometimes works with sisters. In some of these East Indian tribal societies, a man has sexual access to all his wife's sisters. It is preferred that the group of sisters marry the same person, but it is not necessary. The equivalence of sisters is not, in marriage and family relationships, as strong as the equivalence of brothers because women are not the primary property owners and may marry out into many different villages. Hence they do not form a tight social or economic group.

Anthropologist Kathleen Gough reported in 1952 that the concept of fatherhood scarcely existed among the Nayar of South India. She found that every few years in the late 1700s all the immature girls went through a ceremony in which a man tied a "tali" on her, ritually setting free her procreative powers. After that, the girls could have a number of lovers who were determined by caste, not by marriage. When she became pregnant, all her current lovers contributed to the delivery expenses, but none had obligations to the child. Rather, the child was the total responsibility of the mother's lineage. This system minimized the rights of husband and fathers, preserving the matrilineage and emphasizing the child's relationship with the mother's brother. These ideas and customs began to die out in the early nineteenth century as the caste system changed in response to British colonial pressures. With the Pax Britannica, the men spent more time at home rather than in political and military activities. With their reduced obligations to the state, and their reduced ability to make names for themselves as warriors and statesmen, the idea of paternity reasserted itself. In addition, the British colonial government passed a marriage act in 1896 that obliged men to support their wives (instead of brothers supporting their sisters, as in the traditional Nayar system).

Tibet is the center of polyandry. Polyandry is always associated with brothers except in a generation when all the family heirs are daughters. Then the eldest daughter may take as many husbands as she likes, who need not be brothers; the younger daughters are married to sets of brothers in the traditional fashion. Prince Peter found in central Tibet groups of brothers who were allowed to share their fathers' younger wives. He recounted three "typical cases": One noble remarried after his wife's death and shared the second wife with one of his sons by the first marriage; the second marriage led to five more children. The important point was that the property did not have to be split between father and son. In another case, the head of an aristocratic family married off his son to the daughter of a great merchant, and forced the couple to allow him to share the wife. In a third case, a son, when he grew old enough, was invited to share his father's third wife.

Combined fraternal polyandry and sororal polygyny are also known to have occurred among American Indian groups such as the Shoshoni. However, the customs died out so long ago we are not sure how they worked.

Today it seems unlikely that plural marriages will reemerge in the United States even if the tendency to experiment persists. A recent newspaper story, for example, described workshops in Washington, D.C.— where women outnumber men—that instructed women how to share their man with other women. "It beats not having a man," the workshop leaders claimed, and some women seemed to agree. In today's world, polygyny is not economically sound. But now that tests can determine the sex of a child before birth, it is possible that the sex ratio could be disturbed by selective abortion. That might set the stage for some adjustment that would ultimately involve polyandry. A significant change in the economic prowess of women might lead to polygyny. I don't expect to live to see it, but I wouldn't be surprised if it happened.

People know and survive many forms of family and many forms of marriage. Yet, behind the variation the

family—that basic and most elegant of human institutions—is easily recognizable wherever it is found and
whatever shape it takes. The important point is that the
family changes with time and culture. It is subject to
pressures from the economy and polity, from changing
scientific discoveries and religious beliefs. Our wills
and our laws only minimally determine the form the
family will take. The family has forces of its own that
adjust to the real world, and those forces are simply
stronger than our doctrines.

4

The Stations of Divorce

All marriages everywhere end, either in divorce or in death. The death of a spouse may lead to a hard period of mourning, especially if the death was not anticipated. But society helps—the neighbors pitch in, kinfolk gather around, support is provided. That support may be clumsy and intermittent—many widowed persons today feel as if they are ostracized for a period—but it is there.

Mourning at the time of divorce is another story, for which our view of life seldom prepares us. Death of a loved one can be shattering, but death, even when unexpected, is part of what we grow up knowing to be the natural order. Divorce may be a part of social reality, but it is not part of any natural order. No matter how prevalent it is, we are not brought up to plan for divorce as a necessary stage of life.

The death of a loved person may require immense adjustment as the survivors give up some of their roles and take on others, as they adjust their goals and their daily rounds. At the time of divorce, too, literally everything about your life has to be reestablished, even if the marriage had become unpleasant or full of fear and hatred. But the word mourning is rejected by some divorced people to describe their adjustment: they are not sorry the divorce happened, so how could they be in mourning? Yet, over and over again research shows that divorce is both saddening and maddening, even when

the sadness is lightened by relief and the madness miti-
gated by hope.

If you marry for the first time at the average age (24.8
for men and 22.3 for women in the 1980s) and both of
you live to the average expectancy (69.9 for men and
77.6 for women) it will be over 45 years before the death
of a partner. As recently as 1935 it was 35 years. In
England 300 years ago, the figures were from 12 to 17
years for the poor and 22 years for the well-to-do.
Today, despite the prevalence of divorce, a greater proportion of family households remain intact until the
children grow to the age of majority than has ever been
the case. The death rate has dropped more dramatically
than the divorce rate has risen.

As the death rate fell, the divorce rate rose. The two
are not unrelated; people view their lives differently
when they expect to live for a long time than when they
do not. Yet until about 1980 more people were widowed
than divorced, in spite of those high divorce rates; the
two are nowadays about the same. But the chances today
are that the children of most widows and widowers are
adults. Single parenthood and remarriage today are far
different from what they were in earlier centuries. The
major difference (besides the fact that most widows
today are older than they were in the past) is that there
is now likely to be an "outside parent" in the family. In
the last century, almost all the stepfamilies in the land
were created when people remarried after being widowed. Now most stepfamilies, at least those with young
children, are created when the bride or the groom or
both have living ex-spouses. This creates far more complex social repercussions than does dissolution of marriage by widowhood. This chapter is concerned with the
psychological experience of divorce and personal adjustment to that complexity of family forms.

Psychoanalyst Alice Balint once wrote about a six-
year-old boy who formed an attachment to a small dog
while he was with his family on a visit to distant

friends. When it came time to go, he wanted to take the dog home with him. When neither his parents nor the friends would allow this, he turned on it and shouted, "Horrid dog! I don't love you."

What we might call the "horrid dog syndrome" permeates divorce, where it is only a little more complicated than the small boy's experience. Once, you had formed an attachment both to a mate and to a dream of what a happy marriage would mean to the course of your life. In those days, the dream was the guiding vision by which you ran your life. The internal vision would be brought to life with the help of the mate. You were in this together. But as time passed and as you made your choices—especially if you grew away from your spouse in the process—the dream foundered. Yet the dream is dear, and "we" had agreed to it. Or had we? You may begin to question whether the mate ever really did share your ideas. When the dream and the mate no longer fit the life pattern you have created, you are faced with a rough choice: do you opt for the mate or for the dream? Or do you throw them both out and move on?

If you reject the dream, you have betrayed yourself— and it may look as if it's the horrid dog's "fault." At this point, therapy may help some people remodel the dream to fit the real situation. But others may find in therapy only that they cannot make that kind of adjustment; they find the real situation too distasteful. If, on the other hand, you reject the horrid dog, you may be able to retain the old dream, left over from youth. But it may lead you on a lifetime of fruitless search.

In the best of worlds, you remodel the dream in accordance with a surer view of reality, which may mean accepting that the old dream was never more than a wish or an illusion. It may mean accepting the spouse for who that person really is, and then admitting that the two of you are not capable of playing out a dream on which you can collaborate. If you can do that, you can move on to new relationships that are more viable in terms of some new dream.

However, nobody tells you before divorce that you will lose both the dream and the mate, that what is lost in the divorce is not just the relationship, but also the dream, the map of who you are and how you think your life should turn out. Now everything needs reassessment. You have to think not only of where you are, but where you came from and where you are going.

Some people find the emotional upheaval after divorce so disorienting that they simply won't confront it. But not confronting it means not confronting the divorce, which means not confronting the marriage—or your past, your future, or your present life. The post-divorce violence we read about in the newspapers is one way to avoid confronting all these things. Violence is the epitome of the horrid dog syndrome. Violent people tend to deny what they have at one level or another known all along—that their marriage was on the rocks. When the defense mechanism of denial ceased to work, there was no other defense to take its place. Fighting in court is another way to avoid what is going on. Violence gives the illusion that you are in control. But it is always an illusion.

Divorce evokes feelings of loss and rejection. The rejection begins in the marriage. If you reject your dream you compromise your goals. If you reject your mate, you have to explain to yourself why you married this person and stayed with him or her so long, or you have to redefine yourself as having been a fool for all these years. It is a catch-22.

As the rejection goes on (and it seems to matter little whether you reject or are rejected or both) trying to live in a wrecked marriage crushes your self-esteem. Your self-esteem may be thrust even lower when the break-up at last becomes public. You have rejected and been rejected by your former spouse, your "ex-to-be." You are "unchosen" by the one who once chose you and whom you chose, and until recently you were also rejected by a culture that defined any divorced person as inadequate.

The period immediately following the break-up is one of the most ambivalent and unstable most people will ever undergo. Abigail Trafford calls it "crazy time" in her study of divorce. Some people have a feeling of numbness or shock, a psychological mechanism for getting through emotions that are too powerful to handle. If these emotions are allowed to emerge gradually and are dealt with as they come out, the result is healing. If they are never let out, the result may be neurotic behavior later when similar events trigger the original submerged emotions. Some people have gone through the greatest stress during the marriage itself, and have got through much of it before the break occurs. For them, "crazy time" may not be as bad as the last weeks, months, or even years of a bad marriage. Trafford stresses that "crazy time" is normal, and if you don't get through it you become what she calls a "hostage to your past."

Before the 1960s people did not talk about the psychological side of divorce except with the moralistic premise, usually unstated, that they deserved what they got. But, along with legal reform, the 1960s saw increased concern for the psychological situation at the time of divorce and for admitting and examining the way divorced people live.

Morton Hunt's *The World of the Formerly Married*, published in 1968, was the first widely read book about the culture of divorced people. Hunt examined in detail the sexual exploration, the eager seeking for new values, the tenuous bids for togetherness without intimacy. Writers began to use their own case histories as the basis for how-to books. In 1973 Mel Krantzler published *Creative Divorce* (the very title was an idea that, bruited about earlier, was finally coming into its own), which emphasized the wild emotional shifts you swing through during the period just after divorce, and described "nine traps" that might keep a new divorcee from being "creative" about his or her own life—the roadblocks on the journey to the autonomous behavior that goes with deep knowledge of the self: 1. "Unwarranted generalizations," that is, falling for myths about marriage and divorce without examining your particular case; 2. The "self-fulfilling prophecy," being the victim of your own preconceptions; 3. Unreal expectations; 4. Disasterizing, turning your quite ordinary, if painful, experiences into doomsday; 5. Wallowing; 6. Blaming; 7. Flight from oneself; 8. Living through others; 9. "Yearning of the half-person," the idea that you need somebody else to make you whole.

In my own book, *Divorce and After*, in 1970, I emphasized the importance of understanding the components of divorce in order to find order and direction in the emotional chaos. At least six separations must take place, which I called "the six stations of divorce." They are:

1. *Psychological Divorce.* The ex-spouse, as a singularly loved person, must be reevaluated. Even if what you once thought was love has long since turned to hate (or something almost as unpleasant but far more complicated because of ambivalence), the involvement remained intense. Psychological divorce often begins, in at least one of the spouses, long before the break, but it cannot be finished before the break. Psychological divorce is the "core separation."

2. *Legal Divorce.* In our society (unlike some, as we have seen), only a court can give you relief from such obligations as responsibility to pay the debts of the partner or to care for the partner in times of illness. Married individuals are considered in law to be a unit for some purposes, like taxation and property ownership. Only legal divorce can undo the legal unit. That divorce can be obtained only from a court. The legal divorce is the only one of the separations that offers something tangible: you are excused from the legal responsibilities of the marriage and you can get married again.

3. *Community Divorce.* After divorce, both members of the former couple are likely to enter new communities, usually separate ones. Part of the marital community must almost always be given up, and a new community must be acquired.

Many divorced people regret that divorcing the spouse involves "divorce" from their in-laws. "Your in-laws become your out-laws." Many divorced people keep in touch with those they now call "the children's relatives." Some women say that they miss a good and friendly mother-in-law; some men miss the absorption into the ex-wife's extended family. It is sometimes hard to regard this change of community as a process of growth.

In the community divorce, one is thrust back on techniques of making and unmaking friends that one may not have used for a long time. The result is that many divorcees may feel lonely or badgered or both.

4. *Economic Divorce.* The married couple is not only a legal unit, but also an economic unit. At the time of the divorce, property that belonged to the unit that is legally comparable to what jurists call a "corporation aggregate" must be divided into two lots, each belonging to a "corporation sole." This division of property is almost never easy. Since the advent of no-fault divorce, the economic settlement is one of the two greatest difficulties. The other is custody.

The economic divorce may be bitter for several reasons. There is never enough money or property to go around, no matter how much there may be. Equally important, people get attached to certain objects and may need them to support their image of themselves. You may have to construct a new life without your familiar possessions. A divorced person may therefore feel "stripped bare" even if there is no actual change in standard of living.

5. *Divorce from Dependency.* This separation is sometimes said to be part of the psychological divorce,

but I think it is somewhat different from the other stations, because it happens entirely within the self and need have nothing to do with the ex-spouse. Dependency is the failure to be autonomous. A few divorces occur because one or both members have ceased to be dependent and recognize the inadequacy of the marriage. But far more occur because one spouse is fed up with the dependency of the other. In many bad marriages, both spouses have become dependent, usually for support that they should know isn't there, and that they probably do not really need, if they could look objectively at their situation. Indeed, the marriage originally may have been entered into in order to avoid self-reliance and autonomy. One quickly remarried man asked, "You didn't think I'd jump without a parachute, did you?" He is now divorced again, this time without a parachute, so he may make it to his own autonomy. Some people can't make it in only one jump, and a few can't make it at all.

6. *Co-parental Divorce.* This is the most subtle separation of the lot, in part because it can never be clean: the separation of a parent from the child's other parent. Being a single parent is almost always more difficult than being a married parent. Many people in embattled marriages remain good parents, but some don't. When an ex-wife behaves badly, some fathers, however sadly, "disappear." Many divorced persons think the ex-spouse turned not merely against them, but also against the children. When the child, for whatever reasons, fails to live up to the divorced parent's expectations, it is easy to blame the co-parent. As we shall see, more divorces fail in the co-parental aspect than any other way.

Thus, between the separation and the final decree, there are likely to be two people who are angry because they have been rejected in the psychic divorce, they have been cheated in the economic divorce, and they feel misrepresented in the legal divorce. They may be lonely in the community divorce, afraid in the divorce from dependency, and enraged and bitter because they are still tied together in the co-parental divorce. Crazy time, indeed!

When I first began to study divorce in the 1960s, I was interested only in what happens after divorce. But as I talked to divorcing people, I found that they couldn't make sense of their experiences after divorce unless they started way back in the marriage or even before it. Both Abigail Trafford's *Crazy Time* and Elizabeth Cauhape's *Fresh Starts* report the same thing.

Trafford found a trajectory of three stages through which people go in the processes of surviving divorce—crisis, crazy time, and the recovery period. The first two stages are separated by a specific event, the confrontation and break between the mates. The transition between crazy time and the recovery period is more diffuse. Some people can point to a specific incident as the beginning of the recovery period, such as the day they decided they did not have to fight with the ex, or the day they moved out of town to take a new job.

Most people who limp through the crisis and then erupt into the confrontation are not adequately prepared for what they are getting into; they have been entirely taken up with what they are getting out of. Once they are alone, either by themselves or with the children, they are not ready for the rush of frantic emotions, particularly the swings between relief and rage, euphoria and depression. Most people in the period of limbo after the confrontation proceed from an intense pain mixed with joy, which lasts for a year or two.

The conflict with the ex-to-be may actually increase during the period after the separation. This does not necessarily mean that the stress gets higher, but only that the noise gets louder. There has been a lot of rage repressed during the marriage, and it is now coming out. With a few people, the rage becomes uncontrollable.

Some people have not allowed themselves to get

angry during the marriage, and a few will not get angry even after the break-up. Their rage emerges in a masquerade, the most common form being depression associated with low self-esteem. Anger, whatever else it is, is also a mode of reestablishing the self, and if it doesn't spill over into destructiveness, it may even be restorative. Indeed, such rage is destructive only when it destroys its targets or harms the self. It is necessary to live through and understand this anger if you are to get out of crazy time.

A certain amount of "healthy" depression occurs in many people in the crazy time and even after. Guilt often adds to the depression—the sense of being rejected and unloved lies behind both. Depression, if it is not too severe, is one way to avoid both violence and ambivalence. A "suitable" depression—mild enough to deal with and one from which one can emerge, but powerful enough to allow the anger and self-hate to come out so they can be "felt through"—is therefore a valid psychological way to handle these matters. This is not a license to feel sorry for yourself, but depression, properly used, can be the sign of gradual release of terrible emotions.

Falling in love is one way to escape from crazy time, but you must also remember that it may be an important part of crazy time. You may come out of an intensely rewarding affair still having to face the same old crazy time, perhaps made more complex than it was before because you have yet again rejected and/or been rejected.

How do you know when the recovery time is over? The first thing you must realize is that you probably will never completely "get over" it. The point is to adjust to it, to see the ex-spouse calmly for what he or she is, to learn about yourself, to learn how to achieve an intimate relationship with somebody else, whether you marry him or her or not, to deal with what other people think about you and your divorce, and to become a fuller social person by becoming a self-aware one.

Some people can't get through crazy time unscathed. We read about people who kill their spouses and sometimes also their children and themselves during this period. Most of us know people who have toppled over the edge of alcoholism or some other malady when faced with the enormity of taking charge of their own lives.

Although her analysis of the crises in marriage is too simple, Trafford has done the best job so far of describing what she aptly labeled "crazy time." Many people in crazy time overreact either by withdrawing completely from social contacts or, at the other extreme, by throwing themselves into frantic socializing and promiscuity. But Trafford shows that both reactions are normal and even healthy, for, as she puts it, "depression is part of grieving for the past and a sex phase is part of building for the future."

Elizabeth Cauhape, in *Fresh Starts,* describes a smaller and more varied action chain *within* the crazy time. She found that people's reactions to the course of break-up fell into eight categories, which she calls "divorce aftermaths" or "passages." The single process she calls "passage" combines Trafford's "crazy time" and "recovery." The passage is ended when one has a comfortable social identity and an adequate social network.

Cauhape's central criterion is the length of time between the break-up and either a remarriage or settled and intended singlehood. But while she is correct in identifying brief, mid-length, and long passages, a better way to understand her cases would be by the amount and kind of change people can admit, from those who seek a new mate to fit the old patterns all the way to those who contrive utterly new patterns. Most people fall somewhere in between.

The basic aim of people who take a brief passage is to get out of transition—crazy time—as quickly as possible. They usually call it "getting back to normal living." For such people, the craziness in the passage is itself so threatening that they make compromises to reduce it. Among them, Cauhape found three patterns. There are the immediate remarriers who had their plans before they divorced—those who won't jump without a parachute. Another group of short-passage people are "comfortable courters." They want to remarry soon, and set out systematically looking for potential mates who will fit into their old life pattern so that little transitional change is necessary. They change partners, but change as little else as possible. It's one way to get out of crazy time without learning much. Those she calls "graduates" are people who decide that marriage is not for them—they have graduated from marriage. A lot of people say at the time of divorce that they do not intend to remarry, but she has put only those who stick to the course of singlehood into this category.

People who take from two to four years in passage— the middle timers—are of two sorts. The first she calls "steadies." Their goal is to form a stepfamily; they proceed carefully. Courtship often revolves around the children's activities. They are primarily interested in dependability in the next spouse. The other sort are the "enforced remarriers" who marry themselves out of a difficult passage, even when they do not think the new spouse is the optimum mate for them. Enforced remarriers are analogous to young people who marry themselves out of their parents' houses when they are very young.

People who take longer than four years in the passage usually come from longer marriages, held by a sense of duty from leaving their marriages as early as they would have liked. Their major concern is learning about and expanding their own capacities and talents. Such people, perhaps because they are already in a sort of passage long before the formal break-up, are less threatened by crazy time. They know they will not crack if they change their views and their ways. They can experiment with various ways of living. Indeed, they seem to be autonomous people who are not threatened by not knowing precisely where they are or where they are going. Within this group are three types. The first are the "hunters and sorters" who spend a lot of time in the chase. They get involved in a number of temporary relationships; they claim they want to make a good choice and are interested in relationships in preference to casual sex. They often live with new people for periods of time.

Then come the "runners in place," who are socially active and always live alone. They are not totally interested in finding partners now or later, but do not reject the possibility. Sex for them is more casual than for most of the others, even though people in any of the categories may go through periods of casual sex. "Runners in place" like innovation, activity, and discovering themselves; they want to know how they can be different with different people. Their primary involvement is in activities and with themselves. The third group, the "passionate searchers," spend a long time looking for the perfect mate before they remarry. They usually have an immense number of trial arrangements before they achieve what they are looking for, and they enjoy the process.

Perhaps Cauhape's most valuable insight is that divorce shakes up the "configuration of roles." We all play a number of roles in our daily lives. What they involve and how we fit them together help determine what we make of our lives and the kind of people we become. At the time of divorce, people have to rethink and learn to reexperience all of their roles.

The configuration of roles changes dramatically at the time of divorce. It changes again, less suddenly but more dramatically, several times during the passage. All this reminds me of Moussorgsky's "Pictures at an Exhibition," which features a number of pieces, the pictures, set apart by "walking music" as the listener/viewer goes from one picture to the next. Some divorcing people settle in with one picture while others do more walking.

The way a divorcing person handles the transition from one set of roles to another—the amount of anxiety or satisfaction, the degree of self-awareness—is the essence of the passage. With the assumption of new roles and the reformulation of the old ones, the new social person emerges. Some people easily learn the roles first of the separated person, then of the divorced person. Others seem to know them already. Still others seem constantly surprised and take a long time to learn. Some can encompass the roles and get them all into focus, others resist the whole process. Getting your roles straight can be confusing: old ones must be performed as if nothing new was happening; new roles can be contradictory to old values. People have to continue at their jobs and maintain some social relationships while they are learning new roles, and this may lead to exhaustion.

Parenting roles in particular undergo great change. Children influence passage, but seldom determine it. Some of the new roles have to do with taking on necessary tasks that the spouse performed while the marriage was intact, and that can lead to a lot of annoyance. Others have to do with the litigation. Courtship adds still other new roles, almost always unknown because courtship of experienced and divorced people is very different from what it was when the same people were younger, before they married.

Perhaps the most important new role is the one that involves learning about one's self. This is hard to do in a troubled marriage, but it is the essence of the period of passage. And one of the most important dimensions is the willingness to learn from crazy time.

Some divorced people value singlehood. Others find it puzzling or threatening. Some of them use being single as an opportunity to explore their own personalities and they find the state enjoyable, while others can't take the rigors of being alone and autonomous. But most divorced people form new friendships, meet new people, join others of their kind in "the world of the formerly married," and ultimately go into a new family.

Morton and Bernice Hunt note that divorced people soon learn that "there has been a flourishing society of unattached people right under his or her nose all along." This world is full of support groups, escape groups, potential friends and lovers, ideas about how to raise kids as a single parent, and hobbies and other special interests.

Many divorced people are surprised at how quickly they adjust to the sexual code of the divorced, which Hunt and Hunt described as "even faster paced, less inhibited, and more experimental than that of the unmarried young." Studies at the Kinsey Institute have shown that a greater proportion of sexual acts by divorced women lead to orgasm than for the same women during their marriages. This is also the case among widows. The Hunts found that formerly married people are about twice as active sexually in their 1970s sample as their parents' generation were in Kinsey's 1940s samples. Today, compared by age, the divorced are sexually as active as married people, perhaps even more so.

Three-quarters of the men and almost two-thirds of the women in the Hunts' 1977 responses had at least some casual sex after their separations. Divorced people who slept together did so openly. Over half the men and a third of the women did not hide it from their children. Only a decade before, Morton Hunt in his first book had found (and I found the same) that they went to considerable effort to conceal it.

Most divorced people would rather date other divorced people than the widowed or the never-married. They say that many people who were never married do not have enough experience in married life, and that widowed people may act holier than thou because dead mates are unfair competition and because, "You got yourself where you are, but I was pushed into this position by fate, not by fault." Widowed people also for the most part prefer each other.

Yet, some small proportion of the divorced population never again enter the sexual arena. The Hunts found that only 5 percent of divorced men and 7 percent of divorced women had no postmarital sex at all. And whether they are sexually active or not, many divorcees make conscious decisions never to marry again. Some even stick to the decision.

Many divorced people seem to go through a period of "dating around," which the Hunts compare to the *Wanderjahre* of the German apprentice learning his trade. They see a period of casual sex as a mode of restoring the self and note that most formerly married people "outgrow" it. They claim that for most of the divorced people in their sample, postmarital sex is pleasure-seeking on the surface, but underneath serves "the essential ends of ego-repair, the discovery (or rediscovery) of one's mature sexual self, and its integration with the [person's] emergent, changing personality." They divide the process into four phases: ego repair; exploring sexuality, one's own and others, while the idea of love remains threatening; rejoining sex with love; and new deep involvement. They conclude that "if the sexual behavior of the formerly married is hedonistic in intent, it is rehabilitative in effect."

The processes of divorce are difficult but interesting. People who study it are learning more and more about it. People who do it also are learning more as our prudishness disappears and we dare to examine the intricacies of our marriages and divorces.

5

Children:
The Outside Insiders

Since 1976, about two and a half million children a year have lived through their parents' separations. About half of these parents got back together; the other half eventually divorced. In 1980, 12 million American children—17 percent of the total—lived with one parent (92 percent of that number with their mothers). Eighty percent lived with both parents (a figure that unfortunately for social scientists and statisticians, but fortunately for the children, includes stepparents), and 3 percent with neither. Vastly more children than these 12 million have experienced the single-parent household before the parents' remarriages. One household in seven today is a single-parent household. A major study funded by the Carnegie Corporation estimated that four of every ten children born in the 1970s will spend at least part of their childhoods in a one-parent household.

We know appallingly little about the effects of divorce on children, but we have recently learned two sickening facts: because children see the family as *their* world, the inadequacies of the husband-wife relationship are irrelevant to them as long as their own relationships with both parents are "all right." And whereas adults undergoing divorce must mourn a broken relationship, the children mourn what they see as the passing of the family. We can, with no more information than that, understand why children simply cannot approve a divorce unless they have been through so much horror that they themselves have become as embittered as the spouses.

If men and women continue to be good parents and behave politely toward one another in front of the children even as their marriage is falling to pieces, the children are unlikely to know the depth of their difficulty. When the parents finally split, the children seem struck as if by lightning. The most complete study of the children of divorce, *Surviving the Breakup* by Judith Wallerstein and Joan Berlin Kelly, found that "only one third of the children had even a brief awareness of their parents' unhappiness prior to the divorce decision." Even children who had known their parents "weren't getting along so well" had little warning of the magnitude of the difficulty and were not prepared for divorce.

There is more opinion and less fact about the impact of divorce on children than about any other topic that concerns the family. Everybody "knows" divorce is bad for children. Teachers and social workers "explain" depression, temper tantrums, and even delinquency by a child's "broken home." But how much do we actually know? Not much. The first adequate studies to get their information from children are a few articles from the middle and late 1970s by Mavis Hetherington and her colleagues at the University of Virginia, and Wallerstein and Kelly's *Surviving the Breakup* in 1980. A sensitive journalist, Linda Bird Francke, published a book in 1983 called *Growing Up Divorced*, which gives case histories that allow us to examine some children's reactions, and provides good information on how schools treat troubled children at the time of divorce. Marie Winn, in a fascinating book called *Children without Childhood* (1983), examines children's reactions to divorce in the course of a more general argument, also pursued in Neal Postman's *The Disappearance of Childhood* (1982), that childhood is disappearing.

The explanation for why researchers were so tardy in

studying these matters goes back to the 1950s. At that time, Ivan Nye found that divorce was "better" for the children in his sample than was living in a conflicted household. (His study is discussed in Chapter 2.) Today we can see that his finding had an important effect on American attitudes toward divorce. By the early 1960s, divorce lawyers, therapists, and divorcees themselves were telling each other that science had proved that divorce is better for children than a miserable homelife. Very few of them had any idea where the conclusion came from, the size or characteristics of the sample, or how to judge those results.

Many adults latched onto Nye's finding because it allowed them not only to do what they wanted, but to do it in what the courts call "the best interests of the child." Wallerstein and Kelly were led to question that idea by the children they talked with, and they concluded that the reasons parents give for their divorces may not seem "good enough" to the children.

Today's research shows that divorce is good for kids in a few specific situations, especially for children whose parents have subjected them to abuse or who have been yelling constantly at each other or fighting violently. Nye's findings do apply to his sample, and to a few other children. The worst thing for children is to live in an embattled household where there is no comfort or predictability, and children from such homes usually prosper after their parents separate. But it is also "bad for children" to live with parents who continue to battle *after* divorce. It would seem to be battles, not divorces, that cause the problems.

We have learned that the children who suffer most at the time of the break-up are those whose parents have not been violent or bitter at home. (That does not mean that they will suffer most in the long run.) From a child's point of view, the parents suddenly went berserk. In the long run, divorce is probably "all right" for those children whose parents continue to cooperate in their parenting and to retain some respect toward one another. At best, the divorce neither helps nor hinders the child, but is just another vicissitude of growing up.

The ending of the marriage, even with all its pain, may be welcomed by both parents. But children, kept outside the embattled relationship of their parents, cannot feel this way. Husbands and wives in conflict with each other can still be loving and supportive parents. With the split, the child's relationship with each is jolted, and even after they adjust to a new life nothing ever seems the same. The number of children who genuinely wish their parents divorced is small.

Americans have resisted accepting these studies' conclusions. For example, Wallerstein and Kelly have been criticized because they worked with "only" 60 families (even though they studied these families thoroughly). The families were volunteers, not a random sample, which allows some people to ignore the conclusions because they need not be "true" for the whole population. They have been legitimately criticized because they used no control group (which would either have doubled the expense of the study or made the sample so small that other critics would have carped even more). Because their families lived in Marin County, critics have said that the findings in it cannot apply to those who live in Middle America. If we knew more about the children of divorce, all the objections except the last would be more relevant. To date, the Wallerstein and Kelly study is the only one on the impact of divorce on children that is even remotely adequate.

The children with whom Wallerstein and Kelly worked were what they called a "relatively normal group." Before their parents' divorce these children had all been well enough adjusted—they were performing adequately for their age in school and elsewhere. The strength of their research derives from the fact that unlike most psychological investigators of such topics, Wallerstein and Kelly were as interested in the children who were doing well as in those who were having trouble.

These researchers wanted to find out how the children themselves perceived the divorce, and what impact the divorce had on the course of the child's development and maturation. They realized that psychologists and behavioral scientists had never established any norms against which they could compare the responses of the children or parents in their sample. There were not even any standards by which they could distinguish a serious break in a child's development from a temporary regression.

Three-quarters of the children in the Wallerstein and Kelly group violently disapproved of their parents' divorce. Some of them refused to believe what they heard. Some children got angry, screamed and yelled and cursed. Some withdrew. Sometimes the child's reaction to the announcement or the realization was postponed for several days. The self-esteem of many children was psychologically linked with their perception of the self-esteem of a parent, particularly the parent of the same sex. Older boys got upset because their fathers were "thrown out," no matter what the real situation was. Older girls identified with their mother's rage at being rejected. Only 10 percent of the children— almost all adolescents who had seen family violence— greeted the announcement of the separation with relief and approval.

The age of the children at the time of divorce is an important factor in their reactions to it. Wallerstein and Kelly were astonished to find that their sample of 131 children broke itself down into groups that coincide neatly with age and with what psychologists have come to regard as "normal" developmental phases: preschoolers, young school children (6–8), older school children (9–12), and adolescents.

Very young children up to 6 years old are likely to be grief-stricken and uncomprehending. Their primary emotion is fear. Their great concern, either conscious or unconscious, is whether they too can be divorced by one or both parents. Most of them stay with their mothers and miss their fathers. At least a third of them worried about whether their mother would abandon them, and sleep disturbances sometimes resulted from their constant checking to see whether mother was still there. Many of them refused to go to the nursery schools or day-care centers they had attended before. When the custodial parent came to pick them up, they often had a "tantrum of relief."

Young children create fantasies both because they have no facts and because they do not have enough experience to understand whatever facts they do have. A lot of them fantasied that their noncustodial parent had left them and gone off to another family he or she liked better. The fantasies absorb a lot of time and energy, which takes away from the normal processes of development. Wallerstein and Kelly give one poignant example of a father who had not told his 3-year-old about what happened when his mother left because he thought the child could not understand. When the father finally did talk to his son, a lot of questions came out. The father was full of sympathy and attention, and within a few weeks the regression disappeared.

Many young children regress to earlier stages of childhood, giving up what they have already achieved. Toys they had outgrown were taken up again, and there were lapses in toilet training. All these kinds of behavior are signs of stress. Parents find such reactions difficult to deal with because the routine of the household is upset even as they are trying to reestablish it.

Children of both sexes in this age group played in a dollhouse during their interviews, but "no single child was able to relate joyfully to the array of toys with which he or she was presented in the playroom." The play-parents and play-children almost without exception were happy family groups, but some of the children set up families in which the children took care of one another while the adults took care of themselves. A few of them refused to play at all. With the inhibition of play comes a rise in aggression, or an overwhelming fear of the aggression of others.

Children in the next older group, those 6 to 8 years old, have started school. They can be reassured more easily, but their psychological defenses may still be inadequate. These first- and second-graders can take a somewhat more mature view, separating the parents from one another and their relationship with one parent from that with the other.

Children of this age are also frightened and have fantasies about being abandoned and uncared for, including recurring fantasies of being deprived of food. They showed immense yearning for the departed parent; some boys this age urged their mothers to remarry as soon as possible in order to have a father in the house.

These children are beginning to move beyond the family to peers and the neighborhood. But the divorce may create an insecure base from which to reach out. One little boy vastly increased his identification with his father, wearing his father's necktie all the time and talking about his future career in terms of his father's job history. His overidentification was an attempt to strengthen the base.

Many first- and second-graders, when asked to name three wishes, said they had only one—that their parents would get back together. Yet most of them knew it would never happen. Kids of this age can indeed distinguish between their own wishes and the real world. As a result, few of children 6 to 8 expressed anger at the absent father. Instead, they directed their anger at the custodial mother, and the more they missed father, the angrier they got at mother. Anger was also displaced to other people such as teachers and siblings, and the number of temper tantrums increased.

Children in the preadolescent years, from 9 to 12

years old, can more or less understand what is going on, the reality of the divorce and the disruption of the household. But children in this group sometimes told Wallerstein and Kelly's interviewers as truth what they only wished their parents would do. Many turned against the parent they had formerly been closest to. As one reads Wallerstein and Kelly's descriptions, it becomes evident that these children had begun to form the kind of fantasy that we called a "dream" in the last chapter. For them, as for their parents, it was not only the household but the "dream" that lay in ruins. These young people have to get both their parents and their dream back into focus. There is sometimes an almost dramatic search for identity in this age group: they review the ways in which they are related to the parents, or look like the parents.

Nine to 12-year-olds know they are angry, and they know what they are angry about. That anger may lead to activity rather than to depression, to reveling in the new freedom that they have found in their fathers' absence. Others react with a variety of somatic symptoms as defenses against acting out—headaches, stomach aches, cramps, asthma.

Adolescents can understand the situation even more fully, and (perhaps therefore) are even more angry than younger children. Although their identifications are still closely associated with their parents, they are in the process of leaving home and exploring their own sexuality. Their disengagement from parents and from the family as a support structure usually takes place over several years, as they oscillate out of and back into the household. The adolescent depends on family stability to facilitate this back-and-forth. When the household breaks up, those adolescents feel insecure about their home base. As one of them put it, "I was being thrown out into the world before I was ready." Some of them may withdraw and play it cool while others take sides or try to get into the fray.

Adolescent children may, after the break-up, be forced to confront their parents' sexuality in a nonfamilial context. They find it especially difficult if the parents take up with significantly younger men or women, especially if the new partners are very little older than the teenagers and if the parents enjoy activities that the adolescents think of as their own prerogative. Some adolescents felt in danger because their parents were no longer "mature" enough. There was a new kind of competition with the parent, and, at the same time, a loss of security.

In their struggle with their own sexual and aggressive impulses, adolescents often turn on their divorcing parents and accuse them of "immorality." Some of them get somatic symptoms: sleeplessness, fear of being alone, dizzy spells, depression, suicidal ideas. Sexual acting out (as psychiatrists call any sexual act undertaken to express something else) rises with parental separation, especially for girls. Adolescents have heard some of the myths about the inheritability of divorce and they worry about themselves.

Adult children are often infuriated by their "old" parents' divorce. But while they may rage, they usually try not to take sides. They are less likely to try to stop a divorce than they are to try to stop the parents' remarriage, but I know of no study of adult children's reaction to a parental divorce.

The youngest children sometimes think that their own imperfections created the divorce, while most older children can clearly understand what is happening. Wallerstein and Kelly did not find most older children blaming themselves, but they noted that a few of all ages did. One of my students, a university senior, came into my office the morning after he had heard from his father that his parents were divorcing and asked, "What did I do?" My reply was, "You obviously didn't do anything, did you?" He started to cry. Consciously, he knew that his question was silly, but on another level it was relevant to his own survival.

Younger children were concerned about the loss of their father. Yearning for the father apparently had nothing to do with how good the predivorce father-child relationship had been. Indeed, this kind of father-yearning may be typical of our culture and the kind of households we live in; certainly, it is not unique to the time of divorce. The youngsters worried: does father have enough to eat? does he have a refrigerator? somebody to take care of him? a bed? Over half were worried about their mothers—about their health, their capacity to cope, about their depression. Older children expressed similar concerns by talking about the loss of family. A major fantasy of all these children was that the "family" would be restored. Some of them tried quite amazing tricks to bring it about.

Concern about loss of parents has another dimension. At least 40 percent of the children in the sample had poor relationships with their fathers not only after the divorce, but often before. About a quarter of the mother-child relationships were bad. Here the lack of a control group limits the study, for we cannot see how typical these situations are or to what extent they are caused by the adjustment to divorce.

What and when to tell the children is a big problem for parents. One of the first things I discovered when I began to study divorce twenty years ago—and to me it remains one of the most shocking—is that in those days most children were never told anything. Their parents hid behind the cliché, "You can't kid kids, they know something is wrong." But even if they know that "something" is wrong, kids almost surely do not know what it is, and they need reassurance. Just as I had found fifteen years before, four-fifths of the children in the Wallerstein and Kelly sample were never given an adequate explanation of what divorce implied, either in general or for them in particular. Part of the reason that the parents don't tell the children anything is their shame about what has happened. But part is also that the parents themselves do not know enough about divorce in general.

Today, however, instead of being told about the nature of divorce, some children are given the particulars of their parents' experience. Information of the first kind is useful; information of the second kind will almost surely be more than painful. Parents seem not always to understand that children need assurance of continued care; because they are assured in their own minds that the children will be cared for, it does not occur to them that such a doubt might be uppermost in the child's mind.

If parents in the Wallerstein and Kelly study told the children anything at all, they delivered a pronouncement. But it is important that the parents listen to the children instead of, or at least in addition to, making the children listen to them. It takes a lot of sensitivity, and the parents, filled with anger at one another, may not have such sensitivity at that time. Children, distressed themselves and sensing the distress of their parents, usually try not to add to that distress. The only way most of them know to do this is to withdraw and not ask questions. Wallerstein and Kelly conclude bleakly: "No single family in our study was able to provide the children with an adequate opportunity to express their concerns, to recognize with them that the divorce was indeed a family crisis, and that while things were likely to be difficult for a while, the expectation was that life would improve."

Children whose parents are divorcing have to get used to many things. The kind of relationship that is created by "visitation" of the "noncustodial" parent is different from a relationship that is part of the life of a family living together in one household. The division of labor, and hence the core of the parent-child relationship, is very different in a single-parent household than it is in a two-parent one. Such facts—let alone the feelings they evoke—change the relationship of parent and child.

In addition, almost a fifth of the children in the Wallerstein and Kelly study moved to new houses during the first six months after the separation, forcing them to make new friends and sometimes enter new schools. The children of divorce are frequently considerably poorer. Many of them are too young to understand economics, but a few of them know why. In either case, the new situation is rarely explained to them. Money may become the focus of the parents' hostility, and they may fight about medical bills, tuition, and who buys the children's clothes. This makes the children sad and uneasy.

But probably the greatest disturbances in the lives of the children came from the moods and behavior of their parents, as the latter made immense emotional adjustments to the divorce. Adults can use crazy time rage as a focus around which to repossess their own lives, but it can pull their children into an emotional maelstrom.

The children who had the most difficulty were the ones whose parents showed the greatest overt rage. The rage of the parents limits the child's relationships with both of them. It is a father—or, occasionally a mother—caught up in such an emotional storm who is most likely to kidnap the children. Some fathers, on the other hand, will not baby-sit their own children if it will make things easier for the mothers. Either they need to punish their ex-spouses or they have difficulty separating the image of the children from the image of the children's mother. Some of the fathers resist working out arrangements that would give the mother enough freedom to allow her to readjust.

When women fall into emotional chaos, they sometimes try to destroy the father-child relationship; either consciously or unconsciously, they see to it that the father's visitations are unsuccessful. Sometimes they even make it impossible for the children's father to do the job of fathering, claiming vociferously that he is no good because he abandoned the children. Some mothers say to their children, "Daddy left us," giving little or no thought to how the child hears that statement. In this kind of situation the child may feel that he or she has to choose between the parents. Two-thirds of the parents in the Wallerstein and Kelly study competed for their children's allegiance. Even when they didn't, the child usually felt opposing loyalties.

Some parents "assist" the child in using the other parent as the only bad guy. Occasionally, of course, the children are right—in a few divorces there is only one bad guy—but an alliance with one parent against the other is seldom good for the child's maturation. Twenty-five of the 131 children in Wallerstein and Kelly's sample formed such alignments, siding consistently with one parent against the other. Twice as many of that group sided with their mothers as with their fathers.

Children of 8 or 9 or a little older can play important roles at the time of readjustment and are often cast into such roles by a parent. Their resulting feeling of importance makes it easy to "seduce" the child into taking that parent's side. The alignments were usually initiated by the parents. Youngsters from 6 to 12 can be "unswervingly loyal," far more than adolescents who are more likely to involve themselves in their own problems and turn their backs on parental concerns. Among preadolescents, mothers usually found it easier to align their sons and fathers easier to align their daughters. No alignment with a noncustodial parent lasted much more than a year, and all of those who aligned with absent fathers had experienced bad relationships with their mothers before the separation. Alignment with the mothers was stable at a year and a half after the separation, especially if the mother was the custodial parent.

The parents usually realized that such alignments can be damaging to children and broke them off, if they were not themselves too disturbed. Many of these kids act out for their parents. The children get permission from the parent with whom they are aligned to express all the hostility they wish, getting both an "enhanced sense of power" from hurting a vulnerable adult and a reward from the aligned parent. Such an alignment provides a way for kids to split their ambivalence into simple "good" and "bad" parents.

From 15 to 20 percent of divorcing families take disputes about custody into the courts, Wallerstein and Kelly estimate. Francke says that over 90 percent of custody arrangements are worked out by the divorcing parents and their lawyers. Data on this point have never been systematically gathered. Wallerstein and Kelly add that "the adversary proceeding sharpens and consolidates the parents' differences, and once it was initiated, compromise, flexibility, and civilized exchange are neither valued nor possible."

What emerges from all this is that separation and divorce are at least as great a crisis in the lives of the children as they are for parents; that children need support in these periods which the parents, going through their own crisis, are usually in no position to provide. About a third of the children Wallerstein and Kelly studied experienced deterioration in the care they received from parents. The younger children suffered less deterioration than did older ones from about 9 up. Boys of about 9 or 10, and girls somewhat older, felt that their fathers had abandoned them and were deeply hurt. Some of the older girls felt that they had been abandoned by their mothers.

Preschoolers have to get used to spending a lot more time with baby sitters and in child-care homes. Slightly older children have to make their own lunches for school, eat by themselves, and put themselves to bed. Some children find that playmates are not available, not because their parents are divorced (which was what people said as recently as 1963), but because other children's parents won't allow them to play with children who are unsupervised. The result is that two-thirds of the children became more difficult to manage, according to their parents. Younger ones became more clinging, refusing to let the parent-at-hand out of their sight, and the tired parent gets even tireder.

Where do such children get help? The lack of

resources outside the nuclear family is astonishing. Often relatives live at a great distance. Grandparents who live nearby can be immensely helpful (although some of them get so emotionally involved in the divorce that they are not), but most grandparents were not close by. Fewer than 5 percent of the children Wallerstein and Kelly studied got help from the church or a minister. Sometimes there was a helpful neighbor, but not very often. Parents of friends were sometimes among the most helpful people, and these children spent long periods of time with these friends. Pediatricians were never contacted. Fewer than 10 percent of the children got help from any adult.

Children report that they can't share their family troubles with their friends, whose main task is to provide a refuge from the family situation. Particularly little boys used their friends as a way out. Children with siblings said they did not find them very helpful, but those without siblings struck the researchers as more lonely and vulnerable. Older siblings sometimes acted as go-betweens for the younger siblings and parents.

The school was the most helpful institution, probably because it is the dominant one in the lives of most children. It provided secure social organization as well as a refuge. The children in Wallerstein and Kelly's group claimed that teachers were not very helpful, while Francke found that teachers say that they are the only ones the children have to turn to. But she also reports teachers saying they cannot spend as much time and energy on those children as they need without neglecting all the others. Some male teachers become surrogate fathers in the eyes of the boys. One such teacher told Francke, "I feel a tremendous responsibility for them and a tremendous anger toward their fathers. I cannot believe the number of fathers who refuse to parent."

Yet American custom puts the schools in a bind: they must not "interfere" with the family, but they must not allow the children to go down the drain. In over half of

Wallerstein and Kelly's cases the teachers did not know about the divorces; where they did know they tended to hold back from butting into what they considered to be family business. Francke found that the schools and divorced parents were involved in a struggle to redefine the function of the schools, the teachers and principals wanting to provide only formal education, the parents trying to get them to do more. Even as things are, children often feel better and more secure in school than anywhere else.

Perhaps the most important and reassuring single finding of these studies is that the quality of the parent-child relationship does not parallel the unhappy marriage. Even in conflict-ridden households, parents can still be loving and can still support their children's physical and emotional development. A quarter of the children in their sample had what Wallerstein and Kelly called two "committed" parents who were eager to do whatever was necessary for the development of their children. Three-quarters of them were lucky enough to have a mother who was adequate or better, and half of them had an available father who was adequate or better. Although in a quarter to a third of the cases the married pair could not communicate with each other, they could communicate well with their children.

Success in co-parenting often does *not* disappear when the marriage breaks up. Even before divorce—and in some conflicted marriages that never end in divorce—parents can talk about the children, their needs and how best to bring them up. In over a third of the parents studied, child-rearing was never an issue in the disagreements between parents. It is not surprising therefore that some parents can continue to do their co-parenting after divorce.

What Wallerstein and Kelly call the "rational" divorces—those "undertaken to undo an unhappy marriage considered unlikely to change," undertaken with sadness instead of rage, with dignity instead of histrionics, which may actually improve the ultimate situation for the parents—seem *ultimately* to improve the situation for the children. Indeed, women who had had "rational" divorces often wanted to use the new situation as a way to improve the lives of their children. Men, on the other hand, were usually more interested in improving their own lives than those of their children.

In the long run, children of such divorces may see the good of them, whereas children in those households where violence reigned see it immediately. We have to ask whether the old 1950s idea of the divorce being better for children than the conflicted marriage applies in the short run or in the long run. So far, nobody has specifically investigated the question.

Five years after the divorce, many young people have the entire experience under control; others do not. The children who had special problems or had suffered a lot of failures, who (even though they were getting along "well enough") had problems even before the divorce, were made worse by the divorce itself. Any children who doubted the parents' interest in them before the divorce, doubted it even more afterward. The children with the lowest self-esteem were hurt the most.

Although divorce may be a sad and difficult time for children, what matters more than the sadness is whether or not a child gets derailed from going through the stages of personal development. They can recover from temporary regressions; stress and anxiety ultimately go away. But developmental interference may be serious for years to come. Mavis Hetherington suggested as early as 1972 what psychoanalysts had known for years (but, as far as I can find, did not document)—that the psychological effects of a divorce on children may lie dormant and show up only at later stages of development.

Children are indeed insiders in their parents' divorces. They suffer along with the adults, but they do it in their own characteristic ways, dependent in part on their stages of psychological and social development.

At the same time children are outsiders to at least those parts of the relationship between their parents that bring about divorce. As a rule, they stand outside most parental decisions, which they may resent to a degree but come to terms with. Coming to terms with the parents' decision to divorce is a difficult one, yet, again, most children manage it well.

In our society, the household is based on the husband-wife relationship, and that makes divorce especially complicated. For much of the rest of the world, marriage and household are not the same thing. In societies in which the household is based on the father-son relationship, as is often true in Africa, wives join their husbands in their husbands' fathers' households—and remain outsiders. In the case of divorce, the wife leaves and the basic household is undisturbed. In those societies in which the household is built around the mother-daughter relationship, as among the Hopi Indians, adult women continued to live with their mothers, men traditionally moved in with their wives in the households of the wives' mothers—and they remained outsiders. At the time of divorce, Hopi men leave and the households they leave remain intact.

Children are not outsiders in our society as wives are in Africa or husbands among the Hopi. But they are not insiders either, belonging to a household no matter what happens to any particular marriage, as children are in both Africa or among the Hopi. Yet they are insiders in the sense that they have no outside group, no household except that tied to their parents' marriage.

Therefore, it is not just the failure of "the family" that makes divorce so hard on children. It is our household forms. The advantages we feel in being able to set up our own homes can, as it were, come home to roost at the time of divorce. The experience of children at the time of divorce is an integral aspect of our household forms. It is unlikely that we will develop larger households—indeed, every year the size of the average household shrinks as families get smaller and as more and more adults live alone. It is unlikely that the divorce rate will soon go down very significantly. Therefore, we have consciously to build up other, extrafamilial supports for children at the time of divorce. Too often they are forced to bear too much of the burden of the crumbling household.

6

The Successful Divorce

People give many different reasons to explain their divorces, most of them superficial. Nevertheless, when we examine the reasons, what they have in common is that people have ridded themselves of a situation that they think kept them from leading more pleasant and constructive lives. Thus, if after the divorce the people are in fact leading pleasanter and more profitable lives, the divorce was a success. If they are not, it wasn't. But in real life things are never so simple. Sociologist Jessie Bernard said many years ago that every marriage is really two marriages—his and hers. We can easily see that every divorce is two divorces—his and hers. And it's even more complicated than that, for every divorce is many divorces—his, hers, and each child's.

But even if everybody's life is not better, that doesn't mean that the divorce should not have taken place. The marriage itself may not have been the basis of the unhappiness and frustration; perhaps some family members are better off now and others are not. On the other hand, the divorce may have been a mistake. Investigators have found as many as 20 percent of their samples who still wonder some years later whether their divorce had been a good idea. Some people, it seems, have not been any more successful at divorce than at marriage. So it's hard to know what makes a successful divorce.

The idea that a divorce can be successful is relatively new. In the late 1930s, when the nation was aghast that Clark Gable uttered the word "damn" in "Gone With the Wind," the Breen Office (which set and enforced the morality codes for motion pictures) would not allow screen writers to suggest that there might be such a thing as a happy divorce. Today a popular newspaper cartoon shows a mother reading a bedtime story to her child with the closing words, "Then she got single and lived happily ever after."

It is obvious that married people whose difficulties stem from their marriages are helped by divorce. It is just as true, but not so obvious at the time of divorce, that the *only* thing that a divorce can accomplish is ending a bad marriage. If the marriage is not the cause of the problem, then divorce does not help. Psychologically disturbed people, for example, are usually not helped by divorce, although their undisturbed spouses may well be. People whose lives include several sources of stress may end the marriage when that was not in fact the main problem.

Five years after the break-up, according to the Wallerstein and Kelly study, two-thirds of the men and a little over half the women said their divorces had been a good thing. Coming to this conclusion had nothing to do with who had initiated the divorce. About a fifth of both men and women still had ambivalent feelings about the divorce, and another fifth believed that the divorce had been a mistake. Some of the women missed the role of "married woman," while others regretted the financial loss. The divorce was still the central point of the lives of a number of these people, women more often than men. Two-thirds of the divorced parents were still in touch with one another.

On average, men had got out of crazy time and restabilized within the second year of separation. It took the women well into the third year. The healthier the subjects, the earlier they had gotten out of crazy time and rebalanced their lives. About four in ten of the adults in the sample had *not* achieved psychological or social stability in the five years after the divorce. Within that group was a smaller number who had been identified as seriously troubled at the time of the original interviews just after the break-up. In many cases, this psychological instability was chronic and life-long. Most of them had been left by a healthier spouse. Divorce seems to help the spouse and children of very disturbed people, but it does nothing to help the disturbed people themselves.

Most divorced adults ultimately show better psychological functioning. At the time of the original interview, the psychological condition of a third of both men and women in the California Divorce Study was described as excellent. Five years later, that number was larger—half the men and 57 percent of the women. Many neurotic symptoms had disappeared and enhanced self-esteem was evident, especially among the women. Divorce for these people had not only gotten them out of a bad marriage, it had improved their psychological health. They had managed that station of divorce called divorce from dependency and the passages to autonomy very well. The sign that the passage to autonomy has *not* been managed well is the continued presence of rage, especially of bitterness toward the ex.

So, the divorce served a useful purpose for many of these people, particularly women. More than half were better off both by psychological indicators and by their own judgment, and half *that* group were astonishingly better off. Somewhat fewer of the men seem to have used divorce as a device for changing the course of their lives for the better. Particularly those men who had not themselves sought the divorce, but rather had been left, showed that resistance to change characterized their lives.

To determine the success of a divorce for adults, we have to ask, "Was the divorce helpful?" From the standpoint of the children, the question becomes, "Was the divorce ultimately unhurtful?" To put it another way, "Do parents stay with the children and pay the price of putting up with each other, or do they get divorced and let the children pay the price?" Whose interests should predominate? Must divorce be a zero-sum game where a parent's gain is a child's loss, or can it become a game in which everybody is the winner?

The most important of Wallerstein and Kelly's findings about the success of a divorce for children turns out to be simple: the children's development and the way they view the divorce depends directly on what happens to the adults after the divorce—on how successful the divorce is for their parents. If the adults reach a good outcome, then the children make it through the adjustment demanded of them. In far too many cases, when one or both parents cannot achieve a successful divorce, the children pay a very high price. In particular, if the parents continue to fight and blame each other, the children have a difficult time.

Obviously, if parents go through a crazy time after separation and divorce, so do their children. Yet nobody seems systematically to have studied the crazy time of children after divorce. The best information we have is again that of Wallerstein and Kelly. They talked with 131 children just after their parents had separated, although we do not know how long the parents had been contemplating divorce. They interviewed the same children from a year to a year and a half later. At that time, they found that the crises created by the break-up had subsided. Fear and disbelief were no longer present; grief was less acute. Most of the kids had resumed normal development and some had even accelerated. The interviewers talked to the same children a third time, five years after the break-up.

For most of the children, the crazy time was over within a year. A quarter of them said they were far better off than they had been before the divorce. Another quarter, although they still had not fully recovered, were coping pretty well. A small but significant minority of the children—about 15 percent—had not resumed normal growth and development; a few of this group seemed to the interviewers to be even more stressed psychologically than they had been immediately after the break-up. About a fifth of the total group were still anxious, but they were no longer afraid that they would themselves be abandoned. Fewer than 10 percent altogether now thought that their future plans had been scotched by the divorce. Thus, the great majority of children could at the end of a year accept the divorce as a fact. Only a very few of the preschool children clung to the fantasy that their parents would get back together.

When they were first interviewed just after the separation girls seemed to be in slightly better shape than boys. Though the similarities between girls and boys were far greater than differences, the interviewers could determine that girls were a little more skilled at creating relationships with other people, both adults and children. The girls seemed more independent and seemed to play better, but they were also angrier at their mothers than the boys.

A year after the break-up, differences between boys and girls were far more striking, as more boys than girls were still preoccupied with the divorce. The boys held far more tenaciously to the idea that the divorce was a bad thing and should not have occurred. They longed more intensely for their fathers, and felt more rejected by their fathers. More boys were depressed. More girls than boys displayed the extraordinary developmental growth spurts that sometimes occur a year after divorce.

There is some evidence that the girls got better treatment, both from their mothers and from their teachers, than the boys did. It's hard to know what to make of this without a control group, since some educators think that boys are always at a disadvantage in any schools where both sexes are in the same classes because their normal behavior does not fit the classroom requirements of their (usually female) teachers. Boys were more often the targets of their mothers' anger than were girls; a few mothers had turned against their sons because they were like their fathers, and a few simply because they were male. Most of the children showed far more respect for their custodial mother than they had at the time of the divorce, although about a third were still worried about her capacity to cope alone.

Children's relationships with their fathers had changed far more than their relationships with their mothers, probably because their fathers were more likely to be the noncustodial parent. Girls who had good relationships with their fathers before the divorce tended to have good ones after; if the relationship had been bad before, it continued to be bad. Only a few older girls were worried about fathers' welfare.

The boys had a greater adjustment to make. The fathers' interest in their sons grew in some cases; in others the fathers withdrew and all but disappeared from their sons' lives. The number of children who turned against their fathers grew as the age of the children went up. Younger boys were beginning to pull away from any strong identification with their fathers. About half the 9-to-12-year-old boys never turned to and sometimes refused to visit their fathers. One small group of little boys who had well mothers and psychologically disturbed fathers made extremely rapid progress in their psychological growth and development after the divorce.

Most of these kids were not strikingly unhappy at the end of a year. The neediness and the intense loneliness that the interviewers had found just after the break-up was either gone or much reduced. Most of the illness the kids had shown at the time of the separation was gone as well in all but 10 percent of the group. Hyperactivity, stealing, and school misbehavior had not increased.

For adolescent girls, much of the sexual acting out

that had begun when the parents separated had been reduced. One child in four was unhappy and complained about what was happening to the family after the divorce. (Here again, it's hard to know what to make of these findings without a control group.)

Children who were still depressed either had parents who were still angry at each other, or felt rejected by one or both parents. Most of the 10 percent of the children who held themselves responsible for the divorce a year later were still depressed, but some of them had been depressed before the divorce. For a few, whose rhythms of mourning and adjustment were slower, depression that had not been evident at the first interview showed up 12 to 18 months after the divorce.

When boys remained depressed, it was usually because the father had disappeared or visited infrequently, but some boys harbored the idea that their mothers too had rejected them. Some younger boys seemed to be depressed because their mothers were so much poorer after the divorce. Depressed girls, on the other hand, usually had poor relationships with their mothers and seemed more sensitive than the boys to their mothers' psychological state. Younger girls were most concerned with rejection by their mothers, whereas rejection by the father became important only among older girls.

A year after the divorce, the children as a group were far less angry. But a quarter of them—particularly boys and girls who were from 9 to 12 at the time of the divorce, and adolescent girls—were still angry at one or both parents. Some of those 9-to-12 kids were even angrier after 18 months than they had been at the time of separation, and had chosen to cut back their relationship with the noncustodial parent. A vicious cycle developed: the kid was angry because the parent didn't visit, then the parent didn't visit because the kid was angry, so the kid got angrier. Some of this group turned their anger on the custodial parent instead. This problem is by far the worst when the parents continue fighting with one another; their rage seems to generate rage in the children.

At the end of the five years, there was not as much change in the proximity and relationships of family members as the investigators had expected. Half the noncustodial parents still lived in the same county as the children—many within biking distance, even more within an hour's drive—and continued to keep in touch. Not many changes in custody arrangements had occurred, although sometimes a child had gone to live with the father with the assent of the mother.

Twenty-four out of the 60 fathers had remarried; 5 of that number were redivorced, and 2 of those remarried yet again. A third of the 60 mothers had remarried. Two of these were redivorced, and 2 were widowed. Almost half of the children had a new stepmother; most of these also had stepsiblings. About a quarter of the children now lived in a stepfamily. Since a greater proportion of the younger than older women had remarried, the children of these remarried families were more likely to be the children who were younger at the time of the divorce. Only 11 percent of children lived with stepsiblings in their mothers' houses, and only one new couple had had a child. The stepfamily was sometimes felt to be gratifying in spite of the fact that it usually caused some stress. New wives often resented the payments that their new husbands made to support their children, mostly because the payment was made to the ex-wife; they saw and feared it as a way of maintaining the old relationship. Women who marry men with children have to adjust to the fact that those men have to deal with their children's mothers. Jealousy is often hard to control in these situations. But some stepmothers resented even the visits of the children. The San Diego study of stepfathers in the early 1970s turned up the fact that few stepfathers resent the payments made by the natural fathers of their stepchildren; almost all of them said it was the father's duty and hence found no discomfort in it. Some did complain about their wives' relationships with the children's fathers, not so much out of jealousy as that the wives were sometimes "upset" by the natural fathers' actions.

Yet, over half the children reported that they did not find the present situation an improvement over their predivorce family. Almost a quarter said the predivorce family had been "great" while another quarter indicated that the present was a small improvement. The oldest group of children approved of the divorce more often than the younger ones. Now 17 to 24 years old, they could see their parents as people separate from themselves, and could understand what their parents had done. As one high-school senior put it, she would have preferred that her parents had gotten along, but since they couldn't, it was better they had gotten divorced. She could see that both were happier now.

The 9-to-12-year-olds who looked back longingly were the ones who were unhappy in the present. Those who currently experienced an impoverished relationship with the custodial parent, a yearning for their father, or an intense feeling of being rejected, expressed the most disapproval of the divorce. The kids who saw the divorce as a disaster were those left in the custody of an unsupportive, troubled parent and rejected by the other parent. It was not the divorce itself that created that situation, but what happened afterward.

A little over a third of the adolescents were doing very well at the end of five years: high esteem, school competence, friends, good home behavior, and satisfaction. By then there were no sex differences in the way kids coped with divorce—the boys had caught up. Another third of the adolescents were unhappy and dissatisifed. For a few, the unhappiness that had diminished a year after the break-up had reappeared at the end of five years, associated with some new unhappiness in their relationships with one or both parents. These findings may not have anything to do with the divorce; without a control group you cannot tell. For the final third of these adolescents, the adjustment was in the "middle range." They seem to have recovered from the stresses of the divorce but they were considered "average" by their teachers and showed "significant residues" of anger, emotional needs, diminished self-esteem; it is impossible to link this with the fact of divorce. Wallerstein and Kelly's description of this particular third of the adolescent youngsters sounds astonishingly like what some professors call the "B student syndrome": people who have good enough minds, good enough psychological adjustment, good enough performance. Such young people may go any way—some turn out to be brilliant, total flops, or good enough indefinitely. These findings look very much like a normal distribution, although in the absence of precise data we cannot say for sure.

Five years after the separation, most of the fathers were still more or less active in fathering. Almost half enjoyed sufficient visitation so that both they and their children thought they continued to know each other and work together well. Overall, the frequency of paternal visits tended to fall off, but there was no sharp decline, and for a third there was no change at all. The reason for this would seem to be that in the early days of a divorce, time together with the noncustodial parent is more intense, and in longer time periods, than time together when that parent, especially the father, and child are living in the same house. As the children got older, their visits with their noncustodial fathers got shorter but often more frequent, becoming more like those that occur between live-in fathers and their children. These more frequent though shorter and less formal contacts mean that the father can unconsciously adjust far more easily to the child's growing up. About a fifth of the children actually saw more of their fathers as time went on.

Over half the kids were pleased with the general visiting arrangements. Only 9 percent still had no contact at all with their fathers; among these children, the younger ones seemed "capable of waiting indefinitely for the nurturant, loving father," but the older ones responded by rejecting the father.

It takes more than the parent's mere presence at visitation to help (or even to entertain) a child. Some parents even exploit the child—he or she must do housework or something else to serve the noncustodial parent who (often without realizing it) comes to depend on that service. Sometimes the kids spent all weekends doing things the father had chosen to do, and they resented it.

Another difficulty with visitation is that the social relationship between the child and the visiting parent may not change as the child matures. These investigators found the almost incredibly high rate of 15 percent of noncustodial father-child relationships affected by this problem. A couple of children even told Wallerstein and Kelly that remaining childish was the price they had to pay for any relationship at all with their noncustodial parent.

The keys to a successful divorce for kids are: the parents' ability to resolve their own conflicts and put aside their anger; the quality of parenting by both parents and its resumption or improvement soon after the divorce; the personality of the child, as it was formed in the pre-divorce family—intelligence, ability to fantasize, social maturity, and the capacity to turn to other adults or children for help and companionship; and finally, the existence of a support network of friends, especially adult friends, or kin.

To build a successful divorce, adults must learn to see the ex-spouse as a continuing co-parent. This requires a lot of conscious adjusting; there's not much help available from the outside. Perhaps the greatest hurdle comes if the new partners and mates see that concern as unfinished business instead of an ongoing commitment. If new mates are jealous of an ex, if they force choices between themselves and children of a prior marriage, or if they fail to provide support when you try to live up to your responsibilities as a parent, then they are posing more obstacles to a successful divorce.

That last paragraph should not be misunderstood. I am not blaming the new mates/stepparents for anything. I am saying that the mere presence of new spouses can raise old, unresolved emotions and that, as stepparents, the new spouses can add new—and serious—difficulties to the parent-child adjustment if they do not come to understand the situation. If there is competition between the old mate and the new mate, the new mate should know that she or he is in a winning posture, even if the old mate cannot learn that he or she has lost. Old mates may initiate the competition with new ones, but those ex-spouses are only nuisances (however great) if the league between the new mates is strong enough. The only serious problem arises when the person who used to be married to one and is now married to the other has not satisfactorily completed the six separations. Then there may indeed be a game in which one wins and the other loses—until they come to the painful discovery that everybody has lost. To put it another way, marriage is a two-handed game. Remarriage is often a three-handed game.

If competition appears between the new spouse in the role of stepparent and the child, the stepparent should know before marriage that to come between a parent and a child is the most hollow of victories. Here the natural parent is the pivotal player. Of course the child will try to compete. That is a fact of life in this situation. The natural parent may have a hard time refereeing but not taking sides. Sometimes when a child insists on competition or creates as much misery as possible, the new wife/stepmother begins to think that her salary pays the child support to her husband's children who are causing such trouble—an evaluation of the situation guaranteed to make her resent the children, no matter how they behave. Her image of the situation must be corrected: the children may indeed be misbehaving, but her husband is paying that child support to *his* children. Stepparents need a lot of patience—and a lot of wisdom.

Children have a pretty clear view of what constitutes the "good life." Those in the study thought that family life should be stable and without friction, that children should have "enough" contact with both parents and should be loved and approved of by both, and should be free from economic worries. Five years after the divorce, their attitude toward the divorce depended on how well their actual experience in the postdivorce family coincided with those criteria. As it turned out, 28 percent of the children approved of the divorce, 42 percent were in the middle, and a little more than 28 percent strongly disapproved of it.

It is certainly not possible to say that one or two factors cause kids' successful adjustment to divorce or interfere with it. For example, most children who did not see their fathers at all didn't do very well. But some of the children who were visited regularly did not do very well either. "Doing well" was a combination of factors, all filtered through the personality of the child.

I would like to see a study of adults whose parents were divorced when they were children that probed their memories of the divorce and of their adjustment to it. Such a project would be full of traps. One of those traps, one which behavioral scientists always find in interviewing people about things that happened in the past, is that normal people adapt their interpretations of their memories to help them make better sense of the present. Psychologists call this process "working through." Therefore, all statements about the past are bent by present considerations. As historians know well, there is no way to recapture an event without its being attached to somebody's view of it. People's statements about their divorce or that of their parents should not be confused with objective truth. But the way children turn the "truth" of the past into more useful representations of the present would be a sensitive register of the way children adapted. When Wallerstein and Kelly tell us that the children "maintained their loyalty to the pre-divorce family," I think we have to read it as a statement that the children still see the family as psychologically intact even if it is broken into two households.

Two sets of conclusions present themselves, one about adults, the other about children. For adults, it is fairly simple: if they can ultimately emerge from the divorce without regret and with all rage spent, leading satisfactory lives, then the divorce was successful.

For children, successful divorce is more complex. First, children suffer from failed divorces at least as much as from failed marriages. They are often unaware of failed marriages, but they can never be unaware of failed divorces.

Second, what evidence there is points compellingly to the fact that children react badly to stress in their social environments. If a painful and nonproductive marriage provides stress for the children, they do badly. If the stress on the parents is reduced after the break-up, the stress on the child is reduced. But there are two kinds of stress: the stress that comes with crises, and the hassles of everyday living. At the time of the break-up, crisis stress affects everybody, but it goes away as the crisis is resolved; the hassle factor may remain. The hassle factor seems to be more important for the children, the crisis factor for the adults. Both children and adults who survive the crisis, but especially the children, can still be worn down by the hassle.

Finally, the success of a divorce for a child depends on the image that remains of the family. At divorce, a child's family can no longer be taken for granted as just part of the environment. Children have always been telling us, either in words or acts, by their wishes for impossible reconciliations and by their yearnings for absent noncustodial parents, that the family is not destroyed at the time of divorce. But until recently nobody was listening. The family is not destroyed by divorce—but in the past nobody but the children believed it.

Part II

Well Families

7

Good
Marriage

During my interviews with divorced people, both in the early 1960s and twenty years later, I invited them to: "Tell me as much as you like about what happened between the time of your wedding and the time of your divorce." Most of them talked from thirty minutes to several hours, and then often added intimate details after the tape recorder had been turned off. One insightful and terse young woman, however, said only: "We got to know each other." As I look back over all the other case histories, I realize that they all said the same thing. "We got to know each other" is a summary of a good marriage—and also of a bad marriage.

The greater the individual responsibility a person bears for his or her own marriage—freedom in choosing a partner, in letting the relationship grow into a unique union, in allowing the idiosyncratic development of personalities—the more central the relationship becomes to that person's character. That very centrality subjects the relationship to pressures that may lead to destructive dependency on the part of one or both spouses. The more this particular marriage seems unlike every other marriage to the spouses, the more they depend on each other to maintain the uniqueness. Dependability and depending may cross the line into potentially destructive psychological dependency. With work and understanding and good common sense such dependencies need not be crippling, but it takes a special awareness or else a lot of luck.

In American culture, we marry to please ourselves, and each of us wants something just a little different. But in tribal or peasant societies, marriages are pretty much alike because they all adhere to the cultural notions about what marriage ought to be. All are measured by the same scale; the roles in marriage are overt and limited; the nature of marriage is known to all. The strain between the relationship and its social context may be minimal.

Moreover, we Americans can make of our marriages almost anything we like without much feedback from society. People may think these marriages, and us, strange, but they almost surely won't interfere; even parents—perhaps especially parents—and siblings are taught not to. But in Puritan New England it was not labeled interference when the congregation and the neighbors insisted that marriages stick more closely to the approved cultural expectations. Among the African societies in which I worked, the whole neighborhood knew which were "good wives" and "good husbands" because everybody shared the same set of measures, and put a lot of public pressure on "bad" spouses to shape up.

One of the reasons that American marriages are fragile is that no outside cultural norm tells them unequivocally how they are doing. Many of them are riven with misunderstanding. The partners interact with one another at close range, isolated from any audience or any referee. Americans have an immense amount of choice not only in choosing their spouses, but in embroidering the content of the relationship. They pay for that freedom in the greater chances of going wrong when nobody shows them the "right track."

Nowhere else in American culture, perhaps, is the irony of the responsibility that always accompanies freedom as heavy as it is in marriage. As the spouses and the relationship mature, the individual perceptions of the two partners almost inevitably get out of phase. Growing together takes constant renegotiation of basic assumptions and positions. Communication between wife and husband can probably never be so perfect as to bring the two perceptions into constant phase—a popular but unfortunate definition of "true love." Periodic lack of phase is part of growing up: if sometimes you don't get out of phase with yourself, or if one part of your self doesn't occasionally get out of phase with other parts, growing up can't occur at all.

If an American-type marriage is to work, those out-of-phase perceptions have to be brought back into phase. The major block to doing it is the difficulty in knowing when the perceptions are in fact out of phase. But because conflict in marriage is by cultural definition a bad thing, many of us never learn to use conflict positively, to strengthen and enlarge a relationship. We are not supposed to have conflict in a good marriage; we may even, foolishly, make that the definition of a good marriage. Instead of learning from the conflict, we too often make the misunderstanding worse by repressing the conflict so that it can never be dealt with. Unfortunately the repressed conflict does not go away, it seethes. The alternative to making deep discoveries about yourself and about whether your thinking is really in phase with your wife's or husband's, is ending the marriage—either openly by divorce—or else passively by letting it erode into numbness.

Middle-class Americans take it as an inalienable right to marry whomever they choose. During the 1960s and 1970s, many Americans asserted this right by writing their own wedding services, extending the field of choice to include even the content of the vows and the ritual that create the personal marriage. Although drawing up property settlements before marriage has a long history among the wealthy, it became a common practice during that period. People began to make contracts—even deals—about who would do what domestic labor after the wedding, which rights to do what were reserved by whom, and who would get what in the event of divorce.

Given our cultural tradition, which deeply mythologizes romantic love, it is hard even to entertain the possibility that the two principal parties to a marriage may *not* be best qualified to choose their partners, and that the strength of their relationship may *not* depend on the degree to which they personalize it and make it unique. Remember the song in "Fiddler on the Roof" that asks: "Do you love me?" The answer is, "Do I what? I bore your children and washed your clothes!" Compare it with the song in Stephen Sondheim's "Follies" that asks: "Could I leave you?" And the answer is, "Yes."

In traditional African, Chinese, even Mediterranean Catholic societies, the relationship of the spouses is more carefully spelled out and the rights and obligations of each are both more limited and better known to the entire community. The demands for individuality of the spouse are not as great. She can be just "a good wife" without having to be "a good wife for *me*," or he can be a "good husband" without being a special "*my* husband." Marriages in that kind of society are not expected to fulfill as wide a spectrum of a person's needs. And because less is required, the people can settle for less.

When people choose their mates and make their own marriage contracts, they are operating on two levels. First they consciously pick out a person with the "right" qualifications, but when people select their own spouses, the unconscious part of the mind, where wishes live, also enters the process. Its demands by definition are unknown to the self until years later, when the results are in.

So, we make conscious contracts, but more important, we also make unconscious deals. The dogmas of romantic love encourage us to give our unconscious needs practically full control of the process of selection, and that means we select not just to complement our strengths, but to shore up our weak points.

The existence of the unconscious deal as well as the

conscious contract creates a far more complex situation than the one people face when a matchmaker looks for commonly recognized signs of suitability like health, reasonable appearance, willingness to work, a good humor, education, and family standing. There is little if any unconscious dimension to a contract made through a matchmaker. You know better than to expect too much, and you expect fulfillment to come from other relationships, especially from your children.

Most people marry others who are, from a sociologist's viewpoint, like themselves. The mean geographical distance between households in which spouses grow up is only a few miles—until the early 1960s, it was only a few blocks. People marry largely within their own social class. For the first two or three generations after immigration, they even marry into their own ethnic and nationality groups. The conscious contract is usually between a man and a woman of equal social standing and of similar cultural experience. Americans acknowledge this fact largely in negative terms: they say that interfaith or interracial marriages or marriages between spouses of very different ages are more difficult.

So when middle-class Americans pick out a spouse, the results on the conscious level may not look different from what a matchmaker would have come up with. But that's only on the surface. Most middle-class Americans carry about in their heads a lot of ideas of what their spouse is going to be like, amounting to what could be called a job description and a script for the new spouse. These unconscious ideas are related to the rewards and frustrations a person has suffered in his or her past, especially to one's childhood relationship to one's parents. In arranged marriages, the conscious contract, open and known to all, is central. But middle-class Americans marry to enhance their inner, largely secret, selves.

Knowing that each of us makes a kind of unconscious deal, we must ask ourselves: Is my view of my spouse like the spouse's view of herself or himself? Is my view of myself in any way the same as my spouse's view of me? Are my expectations reasonable? Or am I being cast in some drama created in my spouse's unconscious? Am I casting my spouse into roles that I find necessary to populate my internal world, but which have nothing to do with my spouse's view of him or herself in the world? The better we come to know our spouses, the more of the contract may become conscious.

Many people claim that they knew before marriage about those traits in the spouse that eventually led to divorce. We outsiders can see (although they themselves may not) that their unconscious needs blinded their better judgment. It is unfortunate that some people carry on their courtship in a way that keeps them from learning much about their spouses. They are usually the same people who tend to avoid seeing the truth about much of anything.

A viable and long-term marriage is based not only on a successful conscious contract, but on a successful unconscious deal as well. Some unconscious deals lead to neurotic relationships, although the marriages are "successful" at least in the sense that the spouses remain together. Friends, psychiatrists, or even the children of the union may deplore the result, but a neurotic deal for mutual misery can be just as binding as a healthy one for mutual support, esteem, and love.

Every marriage has two heads and two selves. If a couple making love is "a two-backed beast," in the Renaissance expression, then marriage is a two-headed beast. For it to work well, the marriage must also have a set of common understandings, in part derived from the common culture of the spouses and in part built during their interaction. It needs a large area of real mutuality. But it also needs boundaries between the two people as individuals.

Ideally, intimacy in a relationship continues to grow after marriage. But associated with this growth is a trap that catches some marriages. As Bruno Bettelheim put it, "A self, if it is not to wither away, must forever be testing itself against the non-self in a process of active assertion. By self-assertion is not meant a rugged individualism nor an egocentric having one's way. . . . Testing implies both respect and consideration for what we test ourselves against. Otherwise it becomes not a test of self, but of something entirely different, perhaps of brute force.''

Take the case of Toby, who went through two marriages and never drew any boundaries—and neither did her husbands. The first one ran a small but successful appliance store. When she started helping him with the bookkeeping and the billing at the end of the month, they quickly found she was good at it. Soon she was at the store all the time. She took over the sales, and was good at that too. Unknowingly, she forced him into the back room to do repairs. Since she was successful and the business prospered, he would not lay down boundaries against her incursions; he took to drinking instead. She never told him she wouldn't put up with his boozing, but left him without comment. After three years, she married an accountant and went into his office to help with the typing. She was a good typist, began dealing with the customers, and so forth. Her second husband also drew no boundaries, but he took to women instead of booze. Again, she never talked to him about it, never fought with him (her parents had fought with each other, and she declared she couldn't do that), but just up and left with no warning, no renegotiation.

Americans too often get their own autonomy mixed up with selfishness. They are told truthfully that good relationships grow from unselfish loving, but they too often interpret that as forfeiting their own development. If the next steps in their own development seem to be toward greater independence, they may deny their own autonomy rather than erect a boundary between themselves and the spouse. In other words, boundaries must be created between the two selves in a relationship and between each of them and the relationship. The partners must find and keep up their intimacy in the face not merely of constant searching and testing of boundaries, but also, sometimes, of the shock of discovering new ones. Success in marriage is impossible if one self is allowed to swamp the other, or if one dominates the relationship, or if the selves are never sufficiently involved. The more out of phase the two unconscious deals get, the more difficult it is either to reach any consensus or to draw adequate boundaries.

The marriage contract can, in the course of setting and removing boundaries, be changed—indeed, changed almost out of recognition. Recasting the contract is, in fact, the secret of successful marriages, because the unconscious deal may be unstable. The boundaries drawn by a couple in their twenties will almost surely not serve them in their thirties, forties, or fifties.

The changes, however, are not haphazard. They follow an action chain that correlates closely with the stages of psychological development of the husband and the wife. An action chain is a series of "type" events that always follow one another in the same order. In most cases, you don't have to play out the entire chain, it may stop at any point. The action chain of a marriage looks like this:

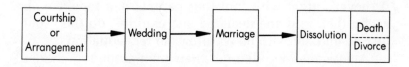

However, for the American middle class, the box marked "marriage" contains its own action chain:

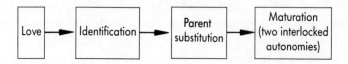

Love: the first phase. Love, late-twentieth-century style, is a combination of friendship and sex. But it is more: in psychological terms, love begins as an exchange of "ego ideals," our innermost images of ourselves, partly unconscious. Our ego ideals grow and change throughout our lives. One basic factor in the ego ideal is our image of our own sex. All of us learn the social roles and cultural activities of both sexes, but we have to forego the opportunity to exercise our talents for playing the roles of the other sex. Those roles are not today as exclusive as they were a couple of decades ago, but a lot of people who are perfectly comfortable being the sex they are still wish they could do some of the things that society reserves for the other sex.

There are qualities in all of us that form a secret or even unconscious part of our ego ideals, but because they belong culturally to the other sex, we do not express them. Then, when we find those qualities in somebody of the other sex, we are attracted: we can love the qualities outside ourselves, in another person. If the attraction can be hooked up with sex, the stage is set for falling in love.

This state of affairs produces character change in both partners. Each not only takes pleasure in loving, but is strengthened and nurtured by being loved. But there may be a catch. The strengthening makes each partner increasingly independent of the demands and rewards supplied by the other. One outcome of the subtle changes that accompany falling in love may be that each envies the other. Each may feel, "I'm giving more love than I am getting" (which may mean, "I give more than I now seem to need, since I have been strengthened by what I have received"). Usually that idea is not expressed in words. But it can erupt into hostility; indeed, it may be just here that "the fight starts." Romantic love and exchange of ego ideals are not enough. If the relationship is to endure, something more has to take over.

Identification: the second phase. Often well before a wedding, and always within a few months after it, another psychological state begins to develop. Each partner identifies with the other. Psychological identification is not just the sympathy of, "I know how you feel." It means taking the partner into yourself in such a way that the other becomes part of your own picture of yourself. You know and consider your spouse's wishes, passions, libido, conscience, pet peeves, and even neuroses; what happens to your spouse creates reverberations in you. The boundary between the two of you is likely to become hazy, and it is just now that the boundary problem can arise.

There are a number of difficulties inherent in psychological identification. One is that you will try to control your spouse by the same methods and for the same reasons that you try to control yourself. Because of the intensity of identification (possibly combined with a fear of some of the forces within yourself or the unreasoning fear that somebody may discover how inadequate you are by looking at your spouse), you may not dare leave your spouse any independence or any area of self-determination.

If the identification proceeds well, the two of you "share the same reality," as psychoanalyst Therese Benedek has put it. The partners experience many things as a couple: "When we were pregnant," or "our career plans." Common ambitions and shared experiences cement the experience of unity but work well only if neither person is sacrificed either to the relationship or to the dream of the other. Giving to the one you love is great, but giving away your self in the process is asking for trouble.

The identification is reinforced from outside as the couple is identified by others as a single unit. Although it is not as stringent as it used to be, the social unit of many activities in American life is still the couple. Anybody not part of a couple may be a "fifth wheel." Both partners may become acutely aware that outsiders judge each of them in terms of the other.

During this phase, the identification can backfire: when you both become aware of being publicly judged in terms of the other, you may regard the spouse as too revealing of those parts of your self that you don't like and that you want to keep hidden.

When this happens, some people look for some flaw in the spouse instead of looking for it in themselves where it may be too painful to confront. In the interests of getting that distasteful identity out of your own ego ideal, it may be easiest to break up the marriage.

If, on the other hand, identification is not distasteful or revealing—especially if it is gratifying—then the marriage is firmer than ever: "How proud I am for people to know that I am married to this wonderful person, whose real quality becomes every day more apparent."

This phase (like every other, but it is more obvious here) is composed of two dimensions: one inside the partners, which involves their identification with each other, and one in the outside world in which each member of the couple takes the other to be the yardstick by which the world examines him or her.

Parent substitution: the third phase. Besides the many changes that parenthood creates in day-to-day life, it is also one of the stages of psychological and social growth. The birth of a child creates a triangle, the eternal triangle. Now, instead of identifying merely with the spouse, each spouse also identifies with the child. Loving the child, knowing you gave it life, that half of its genes are *yours*, creates a new kind of identification. The child seems almost to be an extension of the self. As the child gets older, the parent must learn increasingly to see the child as an individual. Becoming more aware of that fact is part of the maturing process of the parent's identification with the child.

For a parent, the more subtle meanings of identification with the child are profound. When you identify with your child, the child's other parent is thereby identified with your own parent, in or out of conscious awareness. Thus, when a woman identifies with her child, the child's father, to one degree or another, is unconsciously assimilated to her own father. She is, because of that identification, driven to be more like her mother. Likewise, men are driven into an identification with their own fathers. Benedek puts it elegantly: "The marital partners (as if they were parents for each other), become, as once the parents did, a critical forum, a measure of each other's personality."

The difficulties are obvious: any unsettled differences and any unadmitted pain and anger in your relationship with your parents may be turned on the spouse, in some form or another. If all works well, however, the hidden forces of your character are reinforced by the identifications and you are stronger than ever.

Identification with the child or children (and the sex of the child may make a difference in the way a parent readjusts to his wife or her husband) means that the parent goes through the entire process of growing up again—vicariously, but nonetheless intensely. Because you identify with your child and because you play the social role of parent, you have to do the same things all over again, but in the other role. Your own experiences as a child flood back. You have a chance to live them over, and many parents see an opportunity to do it better this time. But obviously you also have a chance to blow it again, and some parents set themselves up to do just that.

The problems of a child of four or five years can, for example, stir the parents' residual Oedipal problems; the experiences of an adolescent child can poignantly bring back the parents' memories of adolescent agonies. If those difficulties were satisfactorily resolved in the parent's own life, then the stirring is helpful in the parental role. But if no resolution was ever achieved, it may make parenting an adolescent trying or even impossible.

Two interlocked autonomies: the fourth phase. When children grow up and leave home, the parents become a couple in a new sense. The role of parent of adult children is not an easy one in contemporary America. The parent may still identify with the children; the successes of the children may remain a major source of pleasure or even of identity. Yet, however much one depends on the children, they are not there—but the spouse is. You have what is called an "empty nest." Many couples love it; a few fall apart, although not nearly as many today as when middle-aged women had fewer options and felt devastated when they ceased to be active mothers.

Being part of an older couple is obviously exciting and rewarding in a far different way from being part of a young couple. Coupleness for the young is based primarily on an exchange of ego ideals, with some emerging identifications. For the middle aged it is built on identifications, some transference from their parents, honest evaluation of their age and experience, and a realistic view of the world.

At this stage of the process, autonomy takes on greater importance. Autonomy is that blessed state in which people choose to be dependent and depended upon for their mutual benefit. You could become independent, but you choose not to. You opt rather for the combination of depending on and dependability. If you can achieve this, then your conjoined ego ideals, identifications and transferences, and your grasp on reality all come together finally and cement the two personalities and the relationship. This state—two interlocked autonomies—must be achieved by each person, but it demands a lot of agreement and communication with the other. If it is achieved, the relationship almost always becomes more solid, even in the face of severe illness or other potentially disruptive factors.

The tasks within marriage, then, are part of a dynamic process: actively building a relationship as you pass through the phases of marriage, and as you draw and maintain your own boundaries. At the same time you constantly adapt both consciously and unconsciously to the other partner, trying to keep in phase and to grasp each new reality as it comes. Such an actively growing marriage proceeds, necessarily, from crisis to crisis. The change points are marked by tension and even by conflict. The crises are closely linked with the growing and developing personalities and with the health and careers of the spouses. Indeed, looked at from the outside, the course of a marriage can be seen as the interplay of the personalities of the people as they continue to develop and to deal with events around them. From the inside, the course of the marriage seems like a process of adapting to the growing and retreating opportunities and demands of the spouse.

American middle-class divorces usually occur in a situation of "multiple crisis." The accumulation of crises puts the partners under great strain. Each must adapt to the new situation, and to the strain itself. Part of a megacrisis may be that one partner says something wounding to the other from which there is no retreat. That may be the precipitating factor that leads the marriage to break up.

At the time of every megacrisis, the marriage "contract" must be reviewed and renegotiated—and the unconscious deal as well. Boundaries must be reexplored, some relaxed, some added, some altered and made more or less permeable.

With each major crisis, with each developmental move, there is a whole new set of role changes, with alterations of basic expectations. If the changed roles and the new expectations are understood by the spouses or are talked about (talking may make it easier for some people, but it is not necessary), then the megacrisis, once past, will probably be looked back on as a "growing point": "We got through *that!*" The relationship is stronger than ever. But if the changes of roles and expectations are not mastered, the crisis point becomes a point of arrest. Growth stops.

An impacted megacrisis can become a permanent block to new solutions of problems that spring up in the lives of the spouses and in the marriage. Whenever there are new difficulties, the old point of arrest suddenly reappears. When a couple hits such a point, either they cannot proceed at all, or they form a sort of scar tissue. They encapsulate the point of arrest and go on. But there is now a "hole" in the developmental path of this relationship. They may agree not to talk about it, but agreeing not to think about it is harder.

Then, at the time of the next megacrisis, something like psychological regression occurs: the relationship whirls back to the point of arrest. Indeed, the new situation may not be a megacrisis by itself. But the new crisis, however it came about, cannot be dealt with on its own terms; it must bear the load of the earlier unresolved crises. After a second or third megacrisis without growth, the load may become too heavy, and the marriage breaks.

Obviously the psychological histories of the partners contribute to these difficulties. Many individuals, in a time of crisis, undergo regressions to difficulties in their infancies or childhoods. Things that happened before the marriage—things that have nothing to do with the marriage—may be dragged in. The spouses may, indeed, drag in problems from previous marriages, or even from their parents' marriages. These often cannot be shared with the spouse, which means that the hole in the relationship grows larger. Such people may not be able, without assistance from psychological counselors, to take the next step in the development either of the marriage or of their own personalities.

All this means that a marriage must constantly be renegotiated. Alienation—withdrawing from the relationship, questioning its character and its content—is from time to time a natural state in any relationship. Alienation may be the only indication that the changes are occurring, a signal that an inquiry is called for. Then only if the renegotiation fails does the alienation in the relationship reach crisis proportions.

Renegotiation may sometimes be difficult. You may not know what you want and your view of your partner may be such that you assign qualities to him or her that have never really been stated or proved. Indeed, your statement about qualities in the other person may be a defense mechanism against looking at your own qualities. But unless you are willing to live as a permanent single, renegotiation is the only game in town. The alternative is to leave your current game and, via the expensive and emotionally devastating route of divorce, get into another one that is just like it. The details of a second marriage may be different, but the moves are the same. And you, the player, are the same, whatever you may have learned the first time around. But everything that you did not learn consciously, you will still have to struggle with, because it's the same old you.

People who renegotiate their marriages successfully seldom know they are doing it. They are the people who made minimal specific requirements in the unconscious deal. They have a good capacity for being honest with themselves, about themselves and about their spouse and their kids. They are able to draw boundaries between themselves and others—and later to reconsider and alter them—so that personal growth continues. They can either talk to each other or communicate in some other way what it is they want and need, like or don't like.

Here is a couple who are now out of phase. He has worked hard and has been successful in business; she has worked hard at keeping a beautiful house and garden and being a gracious hostess. Now in their early fifties, they had raised three successful children, and were rich. When he was offered the presidency of his company, he instead resigned and arranged to work a few weeks a year as a consultant. He was going to live fulltime in the beautiful isolated house they had built for a weekend retreat, and he was going to paint. His inner resources were intact.

But she was in a very different place. She had finished the degree she willingly gave up when she married. Her major was economics and she had long followed the market and sometimes made some money on investments. She wanted to become a stockbroker. He wanted to move to the woods.

These are sensitive and solid people who can talk to each other, so they are working it out. Why shouldn't she stay in the city for a few years and have a career? Why shouldn't he go to the woods? Why shouldn't they meet for idyllic weekends? Why shouldn't they alter their lives to fit their new needs and new situation? They are creative enough that I think they will find a good but nontraditional solution. But since our culture, even today, offers them few guidelines, they are on their own. Far too many couples, faced with this situation, would react with fear, say that their partners were selfish or worse, would limit themselves and their marriage by opting for the traditional view of what they should do, which neither really wants. And then they would pull and tug and hurt and complain until the marriage collapsed, which neither of them wants, or they would grow old and bitter holding it together.

A good marriage offers an opportunity for people to give vital meaning to the life course as they proceed through it. A bad marriage, by definition, limits and cramps the people in it. The course of a marriage is a process of growth, preordained by social context except for style and detail. And yet it often requires a more or less conscious struggle not to drop out and just be what others demand. In societies that do not have these values, a good marriage is not as essential. But for us it is the good life built on genuine knowledge of the self, the partner, and the real world.

8

One-Parent Families

Until the 1970s the main complaint against divorce was that it created "broken homes." We realize today that it isn't so simple. The word "home" in the phrase is misleading because it implies two things: (1) a family living in (2) a household. We have already seen that a divorce does not, cannot, break a family. Therefore, what a divorce does break up is a household. For decades we thought the family and the household were the same thing. Even the demographers of the U.S. Census—who assured me they know better when I questioned them—collect data on *households* and call them *families*.

We don't hear much about broken homes any more. But we do hear about "one-parent families," a term that can be just as misleading unless we define it with great care. Most of what we carelessly call one-parent families actually have two living parents. If a noncustodial parent sees the child and does some important parenting, we can even say that the family consists of two one-parent families. If a living parent has abrogated parental responsibilities—never sees the child and either does not choose to or is not allowed to parent—that is (both socially and, for the child, psychologically) very different than if one parent is dead. Besides, many families with two parents living in the home can nevertheless be one-parent families in the sense that one parent does no parenting. Indeed, you can almost talk about "no-parent families" in those cases in which neither parent pays much attention to the children, no matter what the household arrangement may be.

What we are talking about in this chapter and the next one is the relationship between the family and the household. When the family does not live together in one household, what is the correspondence between the two? How do they fit together? The household is a matter of geography; it can be broken by divorce, among other things. The family, on the other hand, is a matter of kinship. Once a child has been born, husband and wife are a kind of kin, through common descendants instead of from common antecedents, even though they are not what we still call "blood relatives." It is only the force of custom and antiquated laws that keeps us from seeing it that way. One African people I studied expressed the idea by saying that, "Your old wife becomes your sibling." Divorce can cancel a marriage, but it cannot cancel kinship. Not even adoption, for all that it negates the legal rights associated with kinship, can break the genetic ties. Kinship is, at base, a matter of genes; what we might call "legal kinship" is expected to follow the genes, although it doesn't always.

We have already distinguished between one-parent households and one-parent families. One-parent families are families with an "only parent," just as one-child families are families with an "only child." One-parent families can occur in three ways. First, a mother who has never established a co-parental relationship with the father of her children or any other man rears the children herself. One also hears occasionally of fathers (perhaps with the help of paternal grandparents) who take in their illegitimate children who have been rejected by the mother. Second, at the death of one parent, the widowed parent rears the children. Although the children have both a legal mother and a legal father, it is a one-parent family. Third, when one parent abdicates his or her parental responsibilities (whether or not there has been a divorce), and his or her whereabouts is unknown, the remaining family is a one-parent family. We can call these forms the never-married family; the widowed family; and the abandoned family. They all share some problems and each presents unique problems as well. The way you become a single parent has an immense influence on the way you do your single parenting. That is one of the most important points that the sociologist Robert Weiss made in his 1979 study *Going It Alone*. Never-married parents account for about 10 percent of all one-parent households (*not* families).

There have always been women who chose parenthood without marriage. There have also always been more women who did not actively choose, but found themselves with child but without a husband. In 1980 in fact, there were more babies born to unmarried women than at any time in American history, and they made a significant increase in our population growth. One Los Angeles obstetrician reported that about 5 percent of his patients were unmarried women who had no intention of getting married. The age of the unmarried mothers is also significant: 47 percent of babies born to teenage mothers in 1981 (and many of them were very young teenagers) had no legitimate fathers; these girls, as well as the boys who begot the children, were often ignorant of contraceptive methods or else had been unable to apply to themselves an image of being a sexually active adult. But almost one in five—19 percent—babies born by women from 20 to 24 were born to unmarried mothers, and they are not ignorant to the same degree. Almost one in ten—9 percent—were babies born to women 25–29; 7.4 percent to women 30–34; 9.2 percent to women 35–39; and 8 percent to women 40 and older. The social acceptability of the one-parent family has grown enormously. Fourteen percent of those babies were born to mothers with college educations, and 22 percent of the fathers had finished college. That such births occur at a time when abortion is relatively simple indicates that something new is going on. Adoption also is rapidly increasing the number of college-educated single women who start families.

Mothers of illegitimate children no longer sneak away to bear their babies in secrecy and then "give them up." Indeed, babies for adoption are hard to find. According to a 1981 study by Charles Westhoff, a demographer at Princeton University, many of these are not accidental pregnancies, since unintentional pregnancies are way down for all ages 20 and above. More and more of these babies are born to women who want the babies but do not want husbands. The number includes some lesbian women (accurate percentages do not exist) but far more women who are not lesbian. A large number of these women are in their early 30s, and believe that if they do not have a child soon it will be too late.

A fairly small but unknown proportion of these babies result from artificial insemination, usually carried out in doctors' offices, although some doctors (especially in smaller localities) refuse to inseminate unmarried women on the grounds that they do not want to assist in the birth of an illegitimate child. Sperm donors usually sign away rights to any child who is born of artificial insemination with their sperm. The law in the matter, however, has not been fully resolved in the courts. Some insemination centers keep records so that if the child develops health problems—specifically, genetic disease—the donor can be reached for medical history. Far more, however, keep no records at all.

In the early 1980s, several feminist sperm banks got considerable publicity, although most sperm banks have nothing to do with feminism or any other doctrine. The feminist banks are an interesting new development because they indicate that the women who consider men irrelevant in the family—and they may always have existed—have come out of the closet. The prospective mother pays from $100 to $150 to be inseminated; since the procedure often is not successful the first (or even a subsequent) time, the cost may be considerable. She selects the donor from information about his height, coloring, and other physical characteristics, and in some clinics IQ and educational history.

You can even be married and live in a one-parent household if your spouse is permanently hospitalized or imprisoned, or if the second parent has disappeared. These account for only a little less than 6 percent of single-parent households, and as far as I can discover, have never been systematically studied.

One-parent families of widows and widowers make up 14 percent of one-parent households, but the situation is different. Widowed parents often think about what the late spouse would have done or would have approved of, and it can be a source of courage and moral support for both the surviving parent and the children. A widow can say, "Your father would have preferred that . . ." and may even use that kind of admonition as a bludgeon. A widower can point out, "Your mother had decided ideas about. . . ."

A dead parent can become at least as compelling a role model as a living one.

A divorced family is not necessarily a one-parent family. Only when one parent has absolutely given up all parental responsibilities are the problems of a divorced family like those of a widowed or never-married family. Indeed, only then are the problems of the one-parent family less complex (though certainly not less onerous) than the problems of the divorced family.

Most of what are casually and mistakenly called "single parents," however, are divorced—over 70 percent of so-called one-parent households. In by far the most cases, the second parent is still around, and everybody agrees that he or she *should* contribute to the parenting. That idea is a blessing in one sense—it sets a standard, if a minimal one. But it can also be a curse, because the division of parental work has to be worked out. That makes the problems of postdivorce families far different from those of other kinds of families who live in one-parent households.

Households of postdivorce families are more complicated than households of widowed families. In the postdivorce family, the second parent all too easily becomes an "outside influence," that is, outside the household's pattern of decision-making. A co-parent who is outside, especially one who is conscientious and tries hard to be a good parent, may introduce an unpredictable new variable into the way the household is run.

It is important to understand that divorce breaks up households in our culture *only* because we base our households on the husband-wife relationship. When newly married people move into "their own" house, the household thereafter stands or falls on their relationship. The growing relationship between husband and wife is the cement that holds the household together. Americans consider it unfortunate if newly married people have to live with their parents. The norm is most often stated as the importance of privacy and independence, but underlying it is an even more central conviction that every nuclear family should have its own household. We even value it if single people with no children have a home of their own. Yet one of the results is greatly increased difficulty at the time of divorce.

In societies that build households on another relationship—the mother-daughter relationship among the traditional Hopi and Iroquois Indians, for example—divorce does not break households, but merely changes the personnel a little bit. In some societies of traditional Africa, the divorce rate ranges far higher than ours ever has, but the households never change. Those households are based on the father-son relationship, so when a young couple marries, the bridegroom brings his wife into his father's household. Among the Tiv, when I studied them in the late 1940s and early 1950s, 83 percent of the men were either head of their own household in the geographical area occupied by those to whom they traced their relationship solely through males, or else they lived in households headed by their fathers or fathers' brothers. Most of the other 17 percent stayed more or less temporarily with their mother's people.

When a Tiv woman married, she came to live in her husband's compound. When she divorced, she just left. In Tiv custom it was always the woman who initiated divorce. Tiv men told me that it was unthinkable to turn a wife out of her fields and her house, but Tiv men could always ignore a wife or let her go her own way and still lay claim to her sons as followers and collect the bridewealth of her daughters.

The rule about what happened to the children was simple and seemingly always honored: any child who was "still nursing"—in actual practice, boys who were under 5 or 6 years old and girls under about 10—left with the mother, while older children stayed in their father's compound. Those boys who went with their mothers always came back to their father's compound before they reached puberty. Only at home with their fathers did they have full rights of citizens—to a farm, to property they could exchange for a wife. When girls who accompanied their mothers at the time of divorce were ready to marry, usually a few months after puberty, fathers brought their daughters "home" because a woman must be married from her father's house. Daughters often resisted the move, more because they did not wish to marry than because they did not want to go to their father's homes, where most of them had visited, sometimes for months at a time. The Tiv said that splitting a household was always sad and destructive. The emotional tone resembles our disapproval of splitting a household at divorce.

The ways of an African tribe a generation ago provide compelling contrast to the Americans and Europeans, and any other group of people who establish their households on the basis of a husband-wife relationship and who thus experience divorce as breaking up households. Our most cherished institution contains the seeds of its own destruction. And our solution to trouble in that cherished institution leads to even more trouble.

The diagram below shows the various kinds of families.

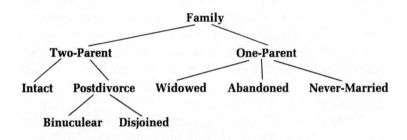

Besides the one-parent families that result from abandonment (with or without divorce), two other kinds of family may be formed at the time of divorce. One, which I call the "disjoined family," emerges when the custody of the children is given to one parent, while the court sets "visiting privileges" for the noncustodial parent. It is still the most common form of the postdivorce family, but it is not a one-parent *family*. The second kind of family arises from a legal award and conscientious exercise of joint custody. It is called the "binuclear family." The disjoined family and the binuclear family will be discussed in the next two chapters. Most of them result from divorce.

No matter what kind of family lives in it, there are three "task packages" (as Robert Weiss called them) necessary to run a family household. The first involves making a living; the second is maintaining the household; the third is child-care. Any one of the three may be a full-time job; certainly the combination of them all is more than one full-time job. Traditionally, the husband/father provided the income while the wife/mother did the household maintenance (with some help from the husband on household repairs and the jobs outside the house). Child-rearing belonged primarily to the wife/mother, with some help from the father in the evenings and on weekends. Children were often assigned household tasks and sometimes helped out with making a living. Policy about child-rearing and child participation in family work resulted from agreement of the parents in league.

In recent years the allocation of tasks has changed somewhat. The practice of hiring servants to assist in the household and child-rearing tasks (which was general among the early New England colonists, and still common among the well-to-do until the First World War) has just about disappeared. Some communes of the 1960s and early 1970s were inventive in finding ways to divide the labor of the household among far more than two people, and still other new ways have been invented to divide the tasks between two partners. Many, especially younger, people say that when both parents share the task of getting a living, the other tasks should also be shared more nearly equally.

Interlinking all these jobs creates a system, dependent on the social relations of all the people in the household. The difficulty comes when the household suffers because the family has suffered. Changing the personnel within a household system affects the totality of the tasks to be done very little. There is still as much to be done. But divorce can affect the identity that sharing tasks in a household provides. "Staying home" is psychologically very different for a married parent and single parent. There is no spouse to share and complement the work of a single homemaker, but only the work itself, which may be—but more likely is not—its own reward.

Children in one-parent households face their own set of pressures. For example, competition between mother and daughter may be more open in a one-parent household: the daughter stays up as late as the mother, and measures her success with boys not just against her mother's success with father, but against her mother's success with men.

Relationships between parents and their opposite-sex children may also become more intense. Single mothers of sons may play out that relationship in the same way they would any other relationship with a male. If they have trouble interacting with men in general, the sons may suffer (an active father could to some degree neutralize such a mother's style). Of course, a woman who has the skill to form good social relations with men may provide her son a magnificent background. Single parents often fear that they can't keep up with the interests of their opposite-sex children. Women who have no interest in sports may start reading the sports page in order to talk to their sons. When such women have difficulties with boy's culture, they begin to think (perhaps mistakenly) that a live-in father would automatically help the boy. We are back to the unconscious contract. Such women may think about what they would *like* their sons to get from a resident father rather than about what the boys might actually get from him.

Ninety percent of one-parent households in our society are headed by mothers. The problems are identical whether the household is headed by a man or a woman, even though their training and preparation in running a household may not be. The only difference I can find is that the community provides more support, and certainly more praise and sympathy, for fathers who succeed than it does for mothers.

Indeed, single fathers have a special problem: their friends and relatives may assume that as men they are incapable of child-rearing, and offer or even force "assistance" on them. Single mothers who could use a little help themselves become furious: "When *he* does an adequate job of taking care of his kids, he is called a superdaddy. When I do just as much nobody notices because that is what mommies are *supposed* to do. No single woman can be a supermommy in the eyes of the world.''

Children living in a one-parent household have actively to learn some things that children living with both parents tend simply to pick up in day-to-day living. One is the nature of ambivalence—how to appreciate and love the strengths at the same time you dislike but accept the weaknesses of the people around you. A child in a divorced household can avoid the difficulties of ambivalence by holding that one parent is right and the other is wrong, by turning all affection on one parent and all dislike on the other. The acute form of this kind of denial leads to what Wallerstein and Kelly called "alignment" with one parent against the other (see Chapter 5). For a child living with both parents, such a division of fault and virtue is hard to maintain.

Another difficulty in one-parent households is that the atmosphere is what one psychoanalyst told me was "desiccated." She went on to say that there is an undertone of healthy sexuality in a well-run household based on a good marriage, and that this undertone is lacking and cannot be supplied in a single-parent household where no signs of parental sexuality are present at all. If, on the other hand, the parent's sexuality is in evidence, it is no longer an undertone and its overtness creates a very different atmosphere for the children. But all other aspects of family life and marriage, this psychoanalyst claimed, can be taught to children who live in one-parent households. The traditional division of labor and traditional attitudes can be discussed; the ways in which the two-person leadership of the traditional households differs from the one-person leadership can be faced and the children told how it is dealt with in other families. Just such discussion about different family customs, throwing their own into relief, would be good for all families.

Sibling rivalry also may take strange turns in one-parent households. Some children assume the role of a missing co-parent, declaring himself or herself to be in league with the parent and hence to be no longer a child. Like most other features of one-parent households, this one has not been well studied.

A most difficult time in a one-parent household comes if one parent—let us take the example of the father—introduces a friend to the children. This can be the first step on the road to the stepfamily. The separated or divorced mother may react violently; ex-spouses may find it difficult not to translate what they feel as an affront to themselves into an affront to the children. This reaction may influence the household, and will certainly influence the children's experience of the two households of their parents.

If the new friend understands her place in the emerging stepfamily, it may be less difficult for the children than for the ex-spouse. Children, visiting their father, struggle to get and keep his attention. If the friend tells him that children should not be given everybody's constant attention, she is missing the point. If she competes with the children, somebody will lose. Only if she can understand why the children demand all his attention, and allows them to have it while they are there, will the children eventually stop competing with her.

There are, of course, two other people involved in this situation. The children's mother has a responsibility not to make her children the avengers of her pride. If she is herself a good mother, her children's relationship with the stepmother cannot damage their relationship with her. The children can, indeed, be doubly blessed— *not* that they will have two mothers, for of course they will not, but they can have a good mother and a good friend in their stepmother.

At the pivot of all this is the children's father. He has to assure his children that his love for them is not affected by the new relationship—and, at the same time, that they can't force him to give up the relationship. If he comes right out and says it, so that the children know he knows what they are doing, and if he assures them that their position with him is not threatened, they cannot do much but accept, whether they like it or not.

Yet the one-parent household may also be free of some pressures of two-parent households. Perhaps the most startling finding in this whole field is that working mothers who are single feel less pressured than do those who are married. Sociologist William Michelson found in a Toronto sample in the early 1980s that single working mothers spend more time with their families, get more sleep, go out more, and get far more help from outsiders than do married working mothers.

One-parent households are not just broken homes, not just unfortunate remnants of some sort of failure. If we stop confusing households with families and one kind of family with another, we can stop blinding ourselves not just to sensible solutions, but to the real problem: inadequate postdivorce parenting.

Today we are beginning to understand that we have a new kind of family, living in new kinds of households that we do not yet know how to run very well. It calls for a lot of social ingenuity. Yet, there is a message in that increasing number of women who plan a one-parent family and who have every intention of taking care of the household in which it lives. The implication is that if we put our minds to it, we can learn to thrive in all these various forms.

9

Postdivorce Families: The Disjoined Family

On Christmas Day, 1983, when police in North Dakota ran a routine check on a man whose car ran into a ditch, they discovered that he was wanted for the abduction of his three-year-old son, Nathan. The police arrested him on the spot and found the little boy safe in a trailer where his father was lying low. The account in the *Los Angeles Times* quoted Nathan's mother: "I think only a parent can understand what it means when your little child disappears. It's a fear, a hopelessness that can't be described." And she added, "I really began to lose all hope, which was the frightening thing." During the four months her son was gone, the mother had, in reporter Josh Getlins' words, "prayed for Nathan's return, bombarded police officials with inquiries and finally hired a private investigator to find her son." We do not know how Nathan felt about it all, but it is likely that Nathan's child psychologist soon will. Nathan has just experienced the gravest problem that besets the postdivorced disjoined family. More and more children are becoming the football in the bitter match between their parents.

The no-fault system of divorce adopted in most states has left the problems of custody untouched. Just as the moral problems of lying and deceit were built into the old divorce laws, so serious problems are built into a legal system that until recently required "sole custody" by one parent or the other. Blinded by the assumption that the only good family is a nuclear family living in a separate dwelling, our custom overlooked the fact that in families of divorce both parents are often willing, even eager, to do the job of child-rearing.

The postdivorce family consists of a father and a mother, no longer married, living in separate households, with the children living with one or the other or in both households. A few postdivorce families become one-parent families because one parent absconds. Most of the rest, however, take one of two forms: the disjoined family that arises when sole custody of children goes to one parent, and the binuclear family that either achieves joint custody or is given it by the court. If the child lives one place and visits the other, it is a disjoined family. If the children actively participate in both households, the result is a binuclear family. Neither the legal nor the residential distinction is always crystal clear, but making an effort to clarify it is useful.

This chapter is about some of the difficulties that beset disjoined families. Although some of its subject matter is grim, it is nevertheless an optimistic account— the problems, at least in their virulent form, can be avoided by any parents who are able to stand back from their own situation to see the effects of their behavior on their children. The most poignant difficulties arise when one parent can do that and the other cannot. Nevertheless, most people, if they understand what their options are and if they can be helped to see the consequences of their actions, can improve the quality of the disjoined family.

At the core of both kinds of divorced family, just as in the nuclear family, is the "league of co-parents."

This league is an essential part of a good family, whether the parents are happily married or are divorced. No matter what kind of household, the league lies at the base of the children's adjustment. If there are two living parents, the relationship between them is a vital dimension of a child's life. When that league is undermined— either by inadequate behavior of one or both parents or by the customs imposed on postdivorce families by courts in accordance with laws that may be punitive to parents and children alike—children have a difficult adaptation to make.

In a two-parent family the parents are "in league" in their efforts to rear their children. Their league presents a united front to the children. It implies that the parents have the children's interests as a primary concern and that they cooperate in creating an environment in which the children can grow up to be happy and healthy. In one-parent families, the parental "league" either was never present or is lost and irrecoverable. Some residue of the league may be invoked by widowed parents.

But in a family of divorce, the league of co-parents has been warped by the dissolution of the marriage. As a result, the parents either may cooperate, at least minimally, so as to maintain some kind of league in rearing their children, or the league may be totally abandoned.

The goal for divorced parents is to maintain or improve the league and to try to assure that it is not affected by the strain of the broken marriage. Some divorced people announce that a co-parent arrangement is not possible. "He should get lost," one woman told me, "we don't like him or need him." You can't help wondering whether she knew the full impact on her children (let alone on their father) of that "we." Some divorced parents claim that continuing the league is not even desirable: "No child can thrive in that situation" (which might mean, "I couldn't bear that situation whether the child thrives or not"). The reason can be stated as a syllogism: my ex-spouse is cruel or dishonest (the rage of crazy time); my ex-spouse is my children's other parent; therefore, my children's other parent is cruel and dishonest. Logical? Yes. True? Probably not.

Many parents and many authorities disagree. They know that good co-parenting can be and often is done in divorced families. When divorced parents can call upon each other for backing, it gives their child a clearer and more consistent picture of what to do and what to expect, and perhaps most important it gives the child the conviction that, no matter what has happened, both parents care.

Today, people ranging from divorced parents themselves to judges and psychologists are coming around to what children have, through their actions and fears, been saying all along: continuing the league of co-parents is the best way to live as a divorced family. And they add, on the basis of their experience and preliminary research, that it works. However, Robert Weiss, in his study of single-parent households in the late 1970s, raised the question: "Does having had five or ten years of shared commitment to raising children together ensure a continued sense of partnership after the marriage ends?" His data told him: "In general, it does not."

Running a postdivorce family demands a lot of trust. If the children are to have access to both parents, at least some trust must be present between them. Unfortunately, the process of divorce itself causes ex-spouses to mistrust each other. To discover whether the distrust is justifiable, ask youself these questions:

1. Is my distrust based on what the spouse did to me or on what (s)he did to our children? If it is both, can I separate the two and discard what was done to me?

2. Has my ex been trustworthy as a parent? If the answer is yes, it should be relatively easy to talk to your ex only as a co-parent, not as an ex-spouse. It takes a lot of thought and patience and self-control, but if you care about your children, it is worth trying.

3. If the answer to the second question is no, was he

or she untrustworthy often, or only once or a few times? Have you talked to the ex about it?

4. Is what my ex does or did to the children actually damaging to them? If so, how can I establish a working co-parental relationship? In the case of Nathan, for example, the father kidnapped the boy four days before he was to stand trial on charges of molesting Nathan's sister. The judge, with the best interests of the child in mind, made the mistake of assuming that Nathan's father was stable enough so that both father and son would profit from continued visitation rights.

Thus, in a few cases a co-parental league between divorced parents may not be possible. There is no easy answer when one parent or both proves to be untrustworthy. Almost as bad, when each parent sees the other as the cause of whatever difficulties the children experience, no league is possible. But that number is relatively small.

Making the postdivorce league work requires giving the children the right to create their own relationships with the other parent; giving the other parent the right to bring up the children as he or she sees fit at the same time that you insist on your right to bring them up as *you* see fit. If there is good communication about it, so much the better, but it isn't absolutely necessary.

Enough studies have now appeared, and enough books by therapists about the people they see, to convince us that the children can adjust to contradictions between mom's way and dad's way as long as there are no face-offs between mom and dad. What children find impossible is the parent who belittles or disallows the other parent's way, for it puts the children into a double bind: they think they have to be "fair" to both parents no matter what it costs *them*. An astonishing number of children explain this clearly by the time they are six or seven years old.

The relationship at the heart of the league of separated co-parents is, in Weiss' words, one "in which each can acknowledge the other's place in the lives of their children, and in which conversations and visits are unencumbered by memories or emotion.'' To reach it, both parents have to have achieved a certain satisfaction with their new lives, which may mean new marriages. If a decent relationship (it need not be cordial, just polite) between the child's father and the new stepfather or between the child's mother and the new stepmother can be worked out, everybody profits. Then, the children will know that two loving parents and one or perhaps two kind and interested and ultimately loving stepparents all are concerned about them.

We do not yet have adequate information about the frequency of co-parental leagues after divorce. We know that the people who have achieved them have found their own way; only in the last few years has any therapist or judge or lawyer offered them help. Within a few years there may be important improvements in what we know about this topic, as social worker Constance Ahrons completes her longitudinal study of communication among ex-spouses, and as other scholars now working on the topic report their findings.

Children in successful nuclear families are vitally affected by, but usually more or less outside of, the parental league. Even then, if the parental league begins to break down, one or both of the parents may make league with one or more of the children. When that happens competition springs up between the child and the excluded parent, unless he or she abandons the family altogether or abandons some parts of the roles of spouse and parent. Psychologists agree that this kind of league between parent and child in a two-parent household may be detrimental to the growth and development of the child. The new league may rob the child of support, may rob him or her of a safe place to grow up.

Unless there is at least minimal success in maintaining the league between the parents, it is likely that one or more children in one-parent households will move into a leaguelike relationship with the custodial parent. That parent turns to one child for the kind of assistance and advice that he or she used to get from the other parent. The child, in a sense, then becomes his or her own parent, and certainly is likely to be a parent-substitute for the other children. The precocious development in children of one-parent households that many observers have noted comes in part from such parent-child leagues. Some psychologists (whose "logic" runs, childhood in "good" homes is not like that, therefore childhood should not be like that in any home) claim that a leaguelike bond between parent and child is unequivocally bad. Others point out that the bond affects the development of the children but not necessarily in a psychologically damaging way. The jury is still out. The question would seem to be, "What does the new form do to or for the children?" rather than "Is it good for children?" Still, if a parent-child league replaces the co-parental league, the structure of the family will be changed, probably permanently.

Those children whom their parents turn into colleagues certainly have more voice in determining the policy of the household than do children whose parents form a league. If a parent-child league emerges, the task packages of the household are again redistributed.

A co-parental league can prosper in all kinds of post-divorce families. In disjoined families, where only one parent has custody, however, it may be harder to maintain. A noncustodial parent, purposely or not, becomes a complete outsider. Or he or she may be turned into what Weiss calls a "consultant" rather than a co-parent, and a consultant need not be listened to. But even good parenting from the noncustodial parent may be resented, especially if it seems to the custodial parent to be more fun than the daily routine, or if it comes at the wrong time. Almost always the situation arises when the two parents do not keep each other adequately informed about what each is going to do with regard to the children. Then, different people have different views of the same events: what seems sensible to one may appear foolish to the other.

Even when a custodial parent approves of what the noncustodial parent does, she or he may resent the other's sharing the upbringing only at a distance and not standing face to face with the daily problems of child-rearing. In such a case, the other's absence may be blamed for a child's problems. "Father absence" was considered crucial by the experts until the early 1970s when it became clear that absence may not be the point, since father can be affectively absent while he is living in the house.

Divorced fathers with custody tend to have the same resentment of their former spouses as parents as do divorced mothers with custody. They complain that the absent mother does not keep in touch with the child and does not make financial contributions to the child's upbringing. Custodial fathers tend—perhaps even more than custodial mothers—to emphasize the child's need for another parent. Weiss found that fathers say that their ex-wives "failed" as mothers and wives out of incapacity, whereas mothers say that their ex-husbands "betrayed" them and the children out of meanness or immaturity.

Recent studies have found that one of the most difficult things for a divorced parent to deal with is the children's feeling of being rejected by the other parent. Many custodial mothers and fathers say that the noncustodial parent visits the children too seldom, and that whatever the parent's reason, children interpret it as indifference to them. Under such circumstances, does the custodial parent stick up for and make excuses for the absent parent? Or do you decide to help the child adjust to the fact that the other parent is being a bad parent? And how do you draw the line between helping the child to accept reality and venting your own grievances? Some custodial parents push the noncustodial parent to spend more and better time with the children, and the noncustodial parent may then feel (perhaps with some justification) that the ex-spouse is using the children to retain a hold.

The co-parents who were having difficulty communicating were neatly summarized by psychologist Persia Woolley in *The Custody Handbook* in 1979:

MOTHER'S VIEWPOINT	FATHER'S VIEWPOINT
1. Overwork, resentment, and worry that the children don't see their father enough.	1. Separation trauma and depression due to loss of family and children.
2. They see him as Prince Charming, while I'm just a drudge.	2. I've become a Disneyland Daddy; my kids are strangers.
3. He runs around and I'm trapped at home.	3. She has the companionship of the kids and I'm alone.
4. He tries to control me!	4. She just won't listen!

As near as Woolley was able to tell, contested custody cases are from 80 to 90 percent of the time between parents who are both fully competent to be custodial parents. Yet, however competent the father, custody is awarded to the mother 85 to 90 percent of the time. These mothers are then saddled with the responsibility for rearing the children by themselves, while the fathers feel devalued and depersonalized. And (remember, we are talking about the contested cases, many cases are never contested because these matters have been worked out) the children tend to feel guilty and defensive about telling anybody that they love either parent, let alone both of them. Thus, our present system far too often leads to symmetrical unhappinesses.

Well into the nineteenth century children were chattels of their parents; as chattels, they "belonged" to their father, as all other chattels did at the time of divorce. Though we no longer think that way, we still behave in custody proceedings on the basis of another kind of stereotype that is just as destructive: women, we say, are nurturers and men are providers. As a result, custody today is one area in which men, by virtue of being male, are still at an automatic disadvantage in the eyes of the law. At the turn of the last century, men automatically got custody, but all that was changed as our concern about children shifted from providing to nurturing, whereupon women automatically got custody. Therefore, until recently the only way a man could get custody was to prove that "in the best interests of the child" his ex-wife had to be denied custody—in short, he had to ruin his children's mother's reputation and play havoc with the children's feelings toward both parents in the process.

It is no wonder that noncustodial parents tend to drop out. In a 1976 study of 48 divorced fathers, psychologist Mavis Hetherington and her associates, Martha Cox and Roger Cox, found that the influence of noncustodial fathers slowly eroded so that after two years there was far less paternal influence in the divorced families than in the control group of intact families. A 1981 study under the direction of sociologist Frank Furstenberg of the University of Pennsylvania found that 40 percent of the children of divorce between the ages of 11 and 16 had not seen their father for over a year and that another 10 percent had seen him only once.

It should be noted, however, that noncustodial fathers *can* become even more involved with their children after divorce than they were before. Wallerstein and Kelly found this true of a quarter of the fathers in their sample. Fathers who stayed away from home to avoid conflict with a spouse may, after separation, take up the fuller relationship with their children that they would have preferred all along.

Fathers who disappear from their children's lives cannot all be blamed as uncaring: some drop out because they have allowed themselves to be convinced, usually by the children's mothers, that they are bad for the children. Fathers who cannot escape from what divorce investigators Morton and Bernice Hunt call the "sham-role" of postdivorce parenting may drop out because of discouragement. Probably the largest percentage, however, cut back because their ex-wives make any contact difficult. In Wallerstein and Kelly's group, one custodial mother in five admitted that she sabotaged the father's visits. More may have done so without realizing it.

A vignette told by Edith Atkin and Estelle Rubin in their 1976 book, *Part-Time Father*, catches the hopeless situation of many noncustodial fathers. A divorced woman, Edith, remarried and moved two thousand miles away with her two children. The children's father, Norman, was enraged at her for taking the children where he could not see them regularly and could scarcely afford to visit them at all. Although bitterly hurt and angry, Norman continued to send money for child support, but eventually Norman too remarried. When money got tighter, Norman guiltily cut back on the amount he sent. After Norman and his second wife had two children, Norman began to miss his payments. His second wife did not hide her resentment at having to economize so stringently because he had to send money to kids he hardly ever heard from. Resentment piled up on all sides. And Norman began to ask, "Why should I deprive my family for kids who don't even care if I'm alive?" He felt shame that another man was supporting his kids, but he salved his conscience with reports that their stepfather was well-to-do, and reasoned that the amount of money it was so difficult for him to send really didn't amount to much. He never heard from the mother of his older children at all any more. He sent his kids birthday cards, but they almost never wrote back, so he stopped writing to them about the time the checks stopped. He gradually forgot about his children; he could recall them only as babies, although they were now in high school. Then he got a letter from his first wife. She asked him to release the children for adoption by their stepfather. The children, she said, wanted to take the name of the man who had raised them. As the authors summed it up, "Everyone is the loser. . . . By default."

Thus, in the disjoined family, the noncustodial parent (most often the father) may be reduced from being a more or less active co-parent to being merely a source of money—and probably, the statistics tell us, an unreliable one. According to data published by the Census Bureau in the summer of 1983, only 46 percent of the mothers who are awarded child support by the courts receive it all. Research for International Women's Year found that fewer than half of divorced women with children under 18 had court-ordered child support payments. And even those who do get all payments lose out to inflation—a loss of about 16 percent in the years between 1978 and 1982. The average child support is little enough in any case: in 1981 it was $2,110 a year; it had been $1,800 in 1978.

In many of the other 54 percent of the cases, the child's father simply refuses to pay. In some, he is genuinely unable to pay, and in others, he disappears. In 1979 some help arrived for mothers who did not get their support checks. Federal computers, including those of the Internal Revenue Service, were used to find the delinquent fathers. Soon after, some lawyers began to specialize in seizing delinquent fathers' property in order to pay child support.

It is significant that the number of fathers who make the total payments rises to 78 percent *if* the fathers agreed through mediation or contract to make the payments. Seldom do noncustodial parents in a disjoined family contribute more money than the court agreement ordained, although active co-parents in a binuclear family are far more likely to help with doctors' bills or other crises.

One source of difficulty is that a man has to give his *ex-wife* money to bring up his children. It might look different if the same man were told he had made an agreement to give that money to the children, with their mother a trustee. As we have seen, the men who are allowed to take an active part in the decisions that affect their children, perhaps even to have some input about how the support money is spent, and who know ahead of time who has to come up with the inevitable "extras" like dentists' bills, have far better records of making their support payments.

Social Security or life insurance or both come to the rescue of the widowed parent, but not the divorced parent. Insurance companies have yet to provide the help to postdivorce families that they have proudly advertised for more than a century to provide for widows and orphans. For the former there is only welfare. While there is no reason that life insurance policies cannot be cashed or borrowed against at the time of divorce, there is also no reason why specific arrangements, based on accurate actuarial tables of risk, could not be written into policies specifically to assist families in the throes of divorce. The need is just as great as in families that are struck by death. There is simply no way to run two households for the price of one, and money is one of the primary problems for almost every divorced parent. Even in two-income families there is not as much money as there was before. The two possible solutions are easier to list than to achieve: members of a divorced family can cut expenditures to meet reduced income, or increase income by the amount required to run two households. The custodial parent in a disjoined family almost always has to cut back most, even when the non-custodial parent feels that he or she is being drained. "Do I have to look for a new job?" "Do I have to find a new baby-sitter?" "Do I have to give up the house and take the kids away from their friends and to another school?'' These worries can bring about something close to personality disturbance for the parent who is unable to provide for the children what she or he thinks parents ought to provide.

The difficulties increase when a noncustodial father remarries and his new wife enters into competition for money with the children of the divorced family. We now have a situation like that of a polygynous family, but we do not have an adequate morality to deal with it. Judges and lawyers report that they are less and less likely to make it difficult for a man to support a second family by granting large support payments to his first family. Obviously, a man's supporting his second family is just as virtuous as supporting his first, so it is hard to work up any indignation over their solution. So the judges add that the mothers of the first set of children should work and share the support.

The public would seem to share the view that the rights of a man's second wife override those of the children of his first. A Michigan study by Ann Goetting in the early 1970s found that people overwhelmingly said that in doling out time and money, a man's second wife should rank before the children by his prior marriage—a stance that troubles me.

But there is something else that troubles me—separating children from parents they want to see and who want to see them. A problem arises because we have two premises in contradiction. One premise says that all children should be treated equally. Another says that a parent and children, especially mothers and children, form an inseparable unit. When the two are in contradiction, the result is too often a stalemate. Today we really do know enough about both genetics and culture to come to better solutions, once we get beyond our stereotypes and our blinders.

Perhaps we need a third premise—that it is destructive for serial wives to enter into overt competition. It is because serial wives see themselves as competitors for resources that this particular social difficulty arises. I realize, of course, that it is not likely that this new stricture will soon be adopted. But, something like it would go to the root of the problem.

So most custodial parents must work, or work more, in order to earn enough money to run their households. Fortunately, work provides more than money; it provides friends and goals. And the marital status of a working mother has become almost irrelevant because most married women with young children also work in the labor force. Yet, single parents, especially single mothers of young children, often experience their time at work overwhelmingly as neglecting their children. A few of them quit their jobs and go on welfare so that they can give time to their children. Their attitudes have not, as far as I know, been compared to those of working married women who can't go on welfare if they quit their jobs.

Divorced mothers, like other working mothers, must rely heavily on day care because the role of breadwinner takes so much time that the role of child-rearer must be given to a nonfamily institution. Good day care is hard to find in spite of the fact that day care has been fairly well accepted by many Americans. Divorced mothers suffer particularly when it is not available.

"Visitation" is a fact of life in disjoined families. The very word is loaded. "Visitation" comes from a Latin term that means "visit for the purpose of inspection." That arbiter of the English language, *The Oxford English Dictionary*, gives as the first of ten meanings: "the action, on the part of one in authority, or of a duly qualified or authorized person, of going to a particular place in order to make an inspection and satisfy himself that everything is in order." Only at the fifth definition do we find: "the action of making a friendly or formal call." *World Book Dictionary* shows that the American meanings are only a little more encouraging. It puts "the act of visiting" as the first of six meanings, but all the rest have unpleasant connotations, including "the visitation of the plague.'' So the word "visitation" marks the relationship between a child and the noncustodial parent as difficult, and the word "rights" means that the law takes the parent's view, not the child's. The terms reflect the court they came from: a visit for the purpose of inspection to which one has a legal right—not the best atmosphere for parents and children to live in.

Nevertheless, the secret of a successful "visitation" is simple. The visiting parent (or, perhaps more accurately but more painfully put, the parent whom the child visits) must keep her or his eye clearly on the parent-child relationship. The visiting parent's own needs must be secondary.

It is important to realize that in a visitation noncustodial parents, particularly those who are conscientious, see their child for relatively long periods of time—all day, all weekend—whereas parenting in an intact household usually consists of more numerous, shorter, and sporadic interactions with the children. Therefore, visitation timing is less "natural," which is even worse if the visits are infrequent, worse if they do not include night stayovers so that the "focus time" can be alternated with periods of just living.

Given the American penchant for "doing something," the task of the noncustodial parent during visitations often comes to be associated in the child's mind with good times and entertainment, often to the annoyance of the custodial parent, who must not only deal with the children every day, but must cope with their let-down after they return from the visitation. Custodial parents may forget that it takes skill for *anybody* to shift from one context to another; for the child of divorce, this switch of context may be particularly difficult and take time.

All this brings us back to the problem of parents kidnapping their own children. The phenomenon is not new. A story in the *Los Angeles Times* on July 24, 1983, told of William Jackson, aged 51, who learned that the mother he had thought dead for 47 years was alive and well. When William was 4, his father took him and his 14-month-old brother away from their home. He told the reporter he had been a "behavior problem" during his entire youth, had no discipline and "shifted for myself all my life."

Kidnapping, then or now, may happen while legal marriages are intact, when one spouse or the other decides just to leave and to take the children away. In at least one in ten such snatches, the parents are married and living together. Indeed, it may be a substitute for legal divorce. Other figures—inadequate, but all we have—indicate that about half of all kidnapped children are snatched between the time of break-up and legal divorce. Kidnapping associated with divorce is likely to occur during "crazy time."

Estimates about the extent of child stealing vary wildly. Journalist Sally Abrahms reports "a Library of Congress Study," not further identified, that estimated 25,000 cases a year. An organization called Children's Rights estimates 100,000, while the estimate of Michael Agopian, who has written a book on the subject, is as high as 400,000 a year. Almost surely the first figure is too low and the last too high. But whatever the number, we have a serious problem on our hands.

Almost all the children who are kidnapped by a parent are frightened. The greatest fright results when children are snatched by a parent who has fought with, and perhaps beaten and injured, the parent who was left. A child's insecurity may be made far greater if he or she is forced to live what used to be called "on the lam." When kidnapping parents take children into hiding, they often use aliases and give the children new names. Children who are made to change their names have identity problems. They cannot share their secrets, so they cannot make friends, and snatching parents usually discourage them in any case.

The kidnapping parent often lies to the child: he or she may convince the child that the other parent is evil or dangerous or dead. Children, especially young ones, usually believe a parent, and it may be years before they know that they were lied to. Kidnapped kids are sometimes told falsely that the parent they have left knows where they are but doesn't bother to get in touch with them. This may mean only that the kidnapping parent has sent messages to the custodial parent saying that if she or he will withdraw the divorce action and come back they can enjoy their children. The snatching parent often demands that the child also lie. Kids who have been brought up to be honest suddenly take new cues from kidnapping parents and can be turned into liars, cheaters, and outlaws.

Stolen kids, in short, are hostages. They behave like hostages, cooperating just as many adults do in that situation. Indeed, it is conceivable that as hostages adults regress to a stage that the children find natural: they look upon their warder as their protector. Kidnapped children also share characteristics with prisoners of war—when the custodial parent or home country does not immediately come after them, they feel betrayed. And they further take on many of the characteristics of fugitives, showing extreme wariness and suffering from sleep disturbances.

Some children don't even realize that calling home is an option. They are told so little, or understand so little, about custody arrangements that they do not know where they are supposed to be. If they are with one parent, they assume that they are in the right place. One boy told Sally Abrahms, "I didn't think of myself as being stolen. I thought, 'My parents are divorced and I have to choose between them, or else one of my parents will decide for me.' I thought that's what happened—that my Dad had decided for me."

Stolen kids don't call home. Many of them, even if they know the telephone number, are too young to know about area codes. And there are always a few kids who don't call home because they want to stay with the parent who has snatched them. Abrahms found cases of children aged 9–12 who called home and hung up without speaking when the other parent answered. They were just checking that the other parent was still there.

The children come to depend on the parent they are with, and this dependency controls their behavior. They are afraid to do anything that might drive that parent away for fear that then no one will be there to take care of them.

Even if they long to be reunited with the custodial parent, most children are afraid of being snatched again. They have already suffered such loss that they fear more. Children, particularly those under 2, do not stop suffering a loss simply by turning their dependency needs to a new person. They may turn to the new parent, but they do not thereby get over missing the parent from whom they were stolen. Sometimes when they realize after coming home that they could have called, children convince themselves that they did indeed try to call when in fact they did not.

Most kidnapped children plot an escape but don't carry it out—it is too risky. If such children actually do run away and report to the police, they are usually taken to the kidnapping parent, not to their custodial parent, especially if that custodial parent is not local.

After the children are returned, the emotional damage done by the kidnapping depends on how long they were away, their ages, how they were treated, the way they are put back into the community of the retrieving parent, and always by their own view of the matter and their own character—how they reacted. They often won't believe that the statements made to them during their captivity are false, or that the kidnapping parent lied to them.

Some children knew that the second parent was looking for them and were pleased, although they did nothing to help the seeking parent. On the other hand, it often takes a child years to forgive a parent for not having come sooner, no matter how hard that parent was trying.

Depression often develops while the child is with the kidnapping parent and may get worse after return to the custodial one. Kids 8 or over recover quickly, particularly if they have professional help, but younger children often don't. Infants, before they are 18 months old, have been subjected to the breaking of a vital bonding relationship; they may recover very slowly if at all. From 4 to 8, the children get the idea that they do not have any control over their lives and must suffer whatever happens to them. Sometimes after a rekidnapping, when the child is glad to see the other parent, it takes several hours to realize what has happened. He or she has again been kidnapped and cannot see the original kidnapping parent: there is going to be more of the same. When they do realize it, the dominant emotion toward the rekidnapping parent becomes rage.

Therefore it is likely to take several months before children can trust the adult with whom they are reunited, and they almost never make a psychological break from the parent who kidnapped them. They may hide the fact that their kidnapping parent was abusive, and lie in order to protect that parent. On the other hand, kids sometimes, to please the parent to whom they are returned, stretch the truth about how badly they were treated by the kidnapping parent. It may take years for any trust in anyone to develop again.

Children who have experienced parental kidnapping are difficult children to parent or even to love; they take out their emotional confusion and rage on whichever parent happens to be with them. They have learned that loving somebody—they were told they were kidnapped out of love—allows you to mistreat them or to demand anything in the world from them. Yet, ironically, after they are reunited with the custodial parent, they still feel they have to be careful to please everybody so they won't be stolen again. They may come to dread seeing the other parent, no matter which one they are with, because they are afraid they will be kidnapped again.

Returned children are often unwilling to go to school, especially if that was where they were snatched. They have sometimes missed months or even years of school, especially if they led a wandering life with the kidnapping parent. When they try to go back to school they feel stupid and out of place, and some of them ultimately drop out.

People who snatch their own children most often say that they do it for their children's sake. They have no idea what snatching does to the psychological development of a child, about the importance of peers and friendship to children, or about what living a lie does to them. They almost always claim that the children have come to no harm with them, and even see themselves as saviors. They think that their children were actually in jeopardy. Parents who are not allowed to parent sometimes kidnap. Parents who have tried through the courts to get what they want and failed may kidnap as a last resort. Some support groups for these people even favor kidnapping if the opportunity to be an equal parent isn't provided. However, an Arizona organization called United Parents against Child Stealing estimated, according to Sally Abrahms, that revenge is the motive in 80 percent of the cases. Abrahms says that about one-third of kidnappers are women, and that the number is going up (her contacts are much wider than mine, but the detectives I talked to said that women kidnappers were very rare).

The reasoning of most snatching parents is selfish and distorted, but based, in some sense or other, on the conviction that the children need them. They hear their children shouting, "Save me!" That is not the kids' message. They cannot realize that it is themselves, not the child's other parent, who is the menace. Abrahms says that as a group they are disturbed and unstable, many with histories of violence. If they weren't before, people who kidnap their kids become con men, adept at forging identity papers to deceive school officials, neighbors, employers, their own children, and ultimately themselves.

Unfortunately, the legal system has until very recently encouraged child stealing. It has finally—at least minimally and sometimes far more—begun to go after fathers who do not pay child support. But it still cannot or will not go after mothers who do not allow legal visitation. It is still not illegal to remove your own child if custody has not been awarded to the other parent. While the couple is still married, or after they have broken up but before custody has been assigned, there is no crime.

Getting the children back takes you into the middle of a legal maelstrom. If the snatcher goes to another state he or she is usually out of range of legal difficulty; if they take the child to another country, they are almost never caught. The parent seeking to recover children may at first try to do it through the courts of the state in which the children are living, which may not recognize the custody decisions of the original state of residence. Kidnapping parents can often get custody papers in the state to which they move so that there are two sets of "valid" custody orders. When they get no help, they may take matters into their own hands.

The FBI looked at child stealing as a domestic affair rather than as a crime until 1982. Now local police must immediately enter the names of all children reported missing into an FBI central computer. In spite of that, police are still often contemptuous of parents seeking to recover children. Abrahms quotes a sergeant from a Missing Persons Bureau in New Jersey as saying, "On a scale of 1 to 10, police rank missing children minus 4."

The high number of kidnappings is in part a reaction to the fact that parents are rebelling against the winner-take-all system of custody. Decent custody and visitation agreements—arranged, if possible, by the parents themselves—may be the only sensible defense against child theft. As long as the noncustodial parent feels as if he or she is being squeezed and nothing can be done about it, this kind of action may result.

The list of things that can go wrong in a disjoined family is, obviously, long and discouraging. We have gone into it at some length not to disapprove of that kind of family but to chart its shoals. Most people who are involved in disjoined families will recognize a few of those shoals and know that the list and its examples are to be taken primarily as a set of warnings. Many of them also know that it is possible to avoid the shoals and have a successful, even a happy, disjoined family after divorce.

There are two alternatives to the disjoined family. The unattractive alternative arises when one parent abandons the children so that they and their custodial parent become a one-parent family. When, and only when, the parent who disappears was truly disturbed or callous, and badgered and distressed the family, can the postdivorce one-parent family be said to be better than the disjoined family. The best alternative is the binuclear family but, as we shall see in the next chapter, it requires two stable and dedicated parents who are willing to give up their geographical mobility and who can manage the intricacies of communicating in a fairly close collaboration in child-rearing. Most parents and children in binuclear families find them better than disjoined families—probably because they work so hard to make them so.

Divorced parents may find themselves in isolated or hostile communities that offer no opportunities for growth so that remaining there would mean remaining a hostage to a family situation that has already proved unrewarding or impossible. They may wisely choose to leave—who of us is adequate to judge? They may find contact with one another so distasteful that they openly opt for second-best. For them what I am calling second-best may be first-best.

There are lots of successful disjoined families, but we do not hear much about them. The horror stories fascinate us; success stories lack histrionics. The requirements of a good disjoined family are the same as the requirements of any other kind of family: parents who try to be what the psychiatrists call "good enough" parents, who create environments in which their children can grow up without too many scarring tribulations; parents who can reach at least minimal agreement about what their children need and how they can get it; parents who look to the interests of their children instead of to victories in their struggles to win something from each other.

As we become more enlightened, as more and more people come to understand the importance of a postdivorce family in the life of children and adolescents, our morality will focus more on values that tell us that divorced mothers must not interfere with paternal visits, that divorced fathers must fulfill their obligations to support (in every sense of that word) their children. As those values grow stronger in the common morality—and in spite of our widespread fears about selfish parents and neglected children who grow up too young, I think these values *are* growing stronger—the vicissitudes of the disjoined family will be somewhat relieved. Insofar as we can learn to do it right, disjoined families can be happy families. Both the people who are in them and the rest of us have a charge to think creatively about how to do it better.

10

Postdivorce Families:
The Binuclear
Family

Ciji Ware, tongue in cheek, wrote that the most difficult thing about sharing custody is socks. "One time I bought ten pairs of the damned things, and in two weeks only two pairs ended up at my house. It was so easy to blame the other parent." But instead, she blamed the sock fairy, who steals one of every pair, and bought some more.

Ware's anecdote illustrates what's needed to make a success of the postdivorce family: patience, flexibility, and good humor. The parents must feel comfortable enough sharing custody with each other, communicating with each other, and sorting their relationships with their children out from their relationship with each other.

Many postdivorce families have succeeded in finding their own ways around what are, to put it bluntly, stupid laws. The term "disjoined family" was used in the last chapter for the kind of family based on sole custody and visitation. Here, we talk about the reorganized family, and use the newer, more positive term "binuclear family." It means that the nuclear family still exists but it is living in a different household arrangement; it emphasizes not the break but rather the, continuity and the cooperation. Social worker Susan Steinman defined it as a family "in which the parents share decision-making authority and child-rearing responsibility after marital separation or divorce, and where the children live in two homes."

The only language to describe the postdivorce family has been negative for so long, so focused on past difficulty, that we overlook both hope and the future. Social worker Constance Ahrons, who coined the word "binuclear," notes that our lack of language may even be the major factor in limiting the kind of relationship that exists between ex-spouses. Therapist Isolina Ricci says we need a new vocabulary for divorced family life to displace the attitudes that have been entombed in such words as "visiting" (try "the children live both at their mother's house and my house"), "the children's other parent" ("my co-parent"), "incomplete home" or "fatherless home" ("two households" may be awkward but will do for a start), "custody agreement" (try "parenting agreement"). We can convince ourselves that divorce turns a co-parenting spouse relationship into a co-parenting business partnership, if that helps.

Common sense and research both show that almost all children want unlimited access to both parents. The only exceptions occur when one parent is alcoholic, or abusive, or severely emotionally disturbed. Wallerstein and Kelly found that the children who saw both parents several times a week made out far better than those who did not. Indeed, several studies have found that children who stay actively involved with both parents are better off physically, psychologically, academically, and socially.

The legal foundation of the binuclear family is joint custody. Joint custody, sometimes called "shared custody," comes in two types: legal and physical. Joint legal custody by itself means that one parent has physical custody, but the "external" parent is still legally responsible for the child in every way. There are two separate households and one parent has "visitation" rights. Joint physical custody means that the child lives with both parents, changing households on a well-understood schedule. The best approach for all concerned is a combination of the two kinds of joint custody. There are several legal ways of achieving something that sounds similar but is different: divided custody means that sole custody moves from one parent to the other on a regular rotating basis (this is also known as "alternating custody"). Split custody means that one child goes to one parent and another to the other parent.

In California and several other states the law says that "there shall be a presumption . . . that joint custody is in the best interests of a minor child where the parents have agreed to an award of joint custody or so agree in open court at a hearing for the purpose of determining the custody." If only one parent wants joint custody, the judge has to cite reasons for not allowing it. Joint custody, in this law, is defined as "an order awarding custody . . . to both parents and providing that physical custody shall be shared by the parents in such a way as to assure the child or children of frequent and continuing contact with both parents." This does not imply automatic joint physical custody. The law forbids denial of the child's medical or school records to either parent.

It is probably impossible to work out good co-parental relationships by means of litigation. It is best done by negotiation (a two-party agreement) or mediation (which involves a neutral third party). The general rule for negotiation by co-parents is to limit the discussions to the topic at hand. The purpose of the mediator is to outline the options and to point out, if necessary, that there may be other options they have not considered. Mediators, unlike arbitrators and far different from judges, have no authority; they cannot make decisions stick.

Indeed, they do not make decisions. Mediators encourage people to look at the privilege of parenting instead of merely its obligations, where the courts are usually stuck. Incidentally, you don't need a legal decree for successful co-parenting or even joint physical custody, although life is easier if you have it. You can always work out your own arrangements. Joint custody proceeds on these assumptions.

According to people who have done it, the best chance to establish a successful binuclear family comes in the weeks just after the separation, before anything is set in legal concrete and before the anger of the separating parents is raised to such a pitch that it overcomes their desire to do well by their children. For people who can master its problems—which fundamentally means mastering their negative emotions toward one another by focusing on their love and regard for their children— it may become permanent.

Three styles of running binuclear families turned up in the studies by Constance Ahrons. First there are the people who consider themselves good friends with their ex-spouses. These people get together as a family every now and then; they have breakfast or dinner together and schedule family conferences; they live close to one another. Such people focus their lives on their children and manage to put their anger with one another on the back burner (where, many such couples find, it cools and ultimately evaporates).

In the second style of running a binuclear family, the co-parents share little beyond parental responsibilities and do not spend time together as a family. Most of their communication is carried on by telephone; they have created clearly established rules for sharing the parenting responsibilities. Their relationship is goal directed and probably, as the children grow up, will phase out.

In the third style, the parents share legal custody but do not share physical custody of the children. They reduce communication to a minimum, getting together only on such occasions as graduations or class plays, when they manage to be polite to one another, but usually do not sit together. In this group, nonresident parents take full advantage of the "generous" visitations, but spend less time with the children than they would in the other forms. The greatest dissatisfaction with the status quo is expressed by this group.

Susan Steinman carried out a preliminary study of children who live in this kind of household in the San Francisco area. Her sample is, she admits, inadequate—only 32 children in 24 binuclear families, all volunteers, and no control group. However, she found several themes that dominate successful (in the eyes of both parents and children) binuclear families: a strong ideological commitment to the two-parent, joint-custody principles; two parents who value each other as parents; parents who value the other parent for the sake of the child. She also found that those who do it successfully have similar views of child-rearing. Their postdivorce anger is muted, in part through the very success in co-parenting. Their sense of loss is reduced by the involvement with their children. Those children most free of trouble were the ones whose parents supported their having a good relationship with the other parent. But if parents had difficulties agreeing on child-rearing procedures, the children were aware of those difficulties and troubled by them.

Running a binuclear family means making practical arrangements. For example, duplicates of some items like toothbrushes can be provided; other items are divided between the two homes; and some items such as cherished toys, sporting equipment, and school books go back and forth with the child. Outsiders must be given both telephone numbers where the child can be reached. Dependable picking up and dropping off of the child becomes essential.

In most cases, Steinman found that the parent who

had the child at any specific moment provided food and entertainment. Expenses such as clothing were shared. Tuition was either shared or paid by the parent with the most income. One set of parents had a joint bank account, into which they put equal amounts to pay these expenses. Medical insurance was covered by the parent whose job provided the best benefits. The tax deduction was alternated. Only 7 of these 24 fathers had a court order for child support, and all of them were fully meeting their obligations (however, they probably would not have volunteered for her study had they not been).

When and how often should the children move from one household to the other? Steinman describes possible variations. Of the 24 families she studied, half used a split-week schedule, which required that parents live close enough together for the child to attend a single school. A quarter of them—again, living close together—took alternate weeks. The other 6 families used a variety of set-ups: changing every day, every two weeks, every three weeks, and in one case every year. Finding the right schedule takes some experimenting. If it is too strict, the children cannot have one or other of the parents when they need them; if it is too loose, neither parent can plan his or her life. Probably the best solution is to create a schedule and then be relaxed and flexible in following it.

The binuclear family is hard for the parents at first. But the major difficulty arises from their reluctance to do exactly what they ought to be doing for their own personal adjustment: repressing their anger at one another as spouses in their common goal of better parenting for their children. Parents who manage to do it find in the long run not only that it makes them far better parents than they could have been in the disjoined family, but also that it works best for them as ex-spouses. There is less postdivorce bickering, less likelihood that grudges will endure, and less court action. Another difficulty for parents with joint custody is that they have to agree to live near one another. This can mean giving up opportunities for professional advancement or remarriage that require moving away.

All students of the binuclear family make one important point: binuclearity does not necessarily mean absolute equality of the two parents. The point is to give the children access to both parents and to share the time and pressures of child-rearing in whatever way works best for the particular family. Children, especially young children, sometimes have trouble grasping the difference between fairness and equality. They feel that they must be absolutely equal in the time spent with their parents and the amount of affection and support they show for each. They usually cannot do it. The child ultimately learns the hard lesson of rendering unto Daddy the things that are Daddy's and unto Mommy the things that are Mommy's. It is, by the way, a lesson that also has to be learned in two-parent households.

The ordinary loyalty conflicts of the two-parent household can become exacerbated in the binuclear family. Indeed, the children's knowledge of their parents' personal sacrifices so that they can have both parents some of the time leaves those children with the emotional burden that Steinman calls "hyper-loyalty." Most children want to reward their parents by doing well themselves, but this can all too easily be turned into trying to see to it that both parents are "happy."

As a successful divorce helps solve the problems in the husband-wife relationship, the binuclear family seems to help solve the problems in the parent-child relationships. For enlightened professionals (therapists, judges, family experts who look to the possibilities rather than to the strictures) and for families themselves, the postdivorce family with two fully engaged parents is now more than ever becoming a viable goal.

Yet the idea of the binuclear family is still fiercely resisted by many people. Some are divorced parents themselves, but many others are not. They insist that a binuclear family demands "head over heart." Of course it does. So does every other kind of family from time to time. Some judges refuse to take what one judge I admire calls "a child's view" of the reorganizing family, so they claim ex cathedra that "human nature" cannot accommodate the binuclear family. There are even lawyers who, reflecting their training and their professional interests, tend to resist the idea of joint custody, thinking it allows their clients inadequate control of the situation.

Some psychologists may tell you, as a parent considering the binuclear family, that you will have trouble achieving your own divorce from dependency if you share custody. For some people, they may be right. But anyone who uses shared custody to get a spouse back is cheating, cheating his or her children. Shared custody must focus on the interests of the children. Other therapists object on the opposite grounds that spousal conflict will overflow into the parent-child relationships. But the point, surely, is that it already does, and joint custody may help keep it under control.

Indeed, some therapists even claim that it is better for children to be separated from one parent than to try to juggle two households. In 1973, Joseph Goldstein, Professor of Law at Yale, child psychoanalyst Anna Freud, and Albert Solnit, a child psychiatrist, published *Beyond the Best Interests of the Child.* Claiming that one parent—either mother or father—should have total control of the child, the authors went so far as to say that the noncustodial parent should have no legal right even to see the child unless the custodial parent approved. Their argument was that consistency was important for the child. The lurking premise was that consistency is more important than a second parent. Since that time studies have stacked up indicating that the greatest advantage for a child after divorce is ready access to both parents who do not demand that the child side with one of them against the other.

The conviction that children will be confused if they have two households is widespread, but the few studies that exist do not bear this out. Steinman found about a quarter of the children in her sample claiming to be unhappy with their two-home system, and this included some complaints about being unable to remember where they should be. One boy put it, "the big problem with joint custody is that you have to remember where the spoons are." Half of these were very young and the confusion was not totally inappropriate for their age. For the others, anxiety seemed to stem from unresolved worries about their parents' separation.

The rest of the children themselves said that everybody else may be confused, but they were not. Until we get such a control group, we can safely assume that for one child in four to be "confused and annoyed" is not an unusual number even in nuclear families—there is a possibility that the number of confused children in nuclear families may be even larger.

The binuclear family, if you can do it, is a better form than the disjoined family. But, if you can't do it, it is well to remember that disjoined families too can work for members. Only in a totally unsuccessful divorce does the ex-spouse relationship deteriorate so far that parenting on at least one side is made so difficult that a completely broken family results.

If the requirements of binuclear living seem heavier to the people who live with them, it is in part because there is no norm—each binuclear family is forging new rules. People in binuclear families consciously think and talk far more about family relationships than do those in simple nuclear households, and as a result tend to be wiser about them. Whenever difficulties emerge, everyone is instantly aware of them. Little comes naturally in binuclear households, but social scientists know that not much comes naturally in *any* household. It has all been learned.

The children in Steinman's group of binuclear families accepted the present situation, by and large, with good grace. However, all of them wished that they could have had an intact household. They were less insecure and fearful than the children Wallerstein and Kelly studied, but just as likely to imagine that their parents would get back together. Indeed, Steinman suggests that the very fact that the parents can cooperate in co-parenting may keep alive the children's fantasies of their parents' remarriage, which some people think is the worst thing about binuclear families.

The binuclear family is not a panacea. But no form of family can ever be totally satisfactory for everybody in it all the time. Over half the children in Steinman's sample had been in binuclear families for over half of their lives. They had learned two things clearly: that their parents had gone to a lot of trouble and made a lot of sacrifices so that they could continue to have both parents, and that each was the complete parent during the time the child stayed with him or her.

Mel Roman and William Haddad, in a 1978 book called *The Disposable Parent*, claimed that it would take a revolution to convince people that joint custody is psychologically sound for children and practical for parents. Only six years later, this revolution is already starting, although some people haven't heard about it yet and others are diehards. The greatest barriers that remain are people's ideas about themselves and their options.

11

The
Stepfamily

Stepfamilies have been around for centuries, but the stepfamilies we form today are far more complicated than most of the earlier ones. In the old days, stepfamilies were based on remarriage after the death of a spouse. Today, when most stepfamilies occur after divorce, most remarrying parents are already members of families—families that have everything in them but a marriage. Many remarried parents today are involved in two co-parental leagues—one in a stepfamily and one in a postdivorce family. They are sometimes confused by these two families with their overlapping membership, which sometimes seem opposed to one another. Even more important, most children already have a family, and for that reason they may experience the stepfamily as a complication. They may also, even at the same time, experience it as an immense pleasure.

To handle multiple family membership, people need special information and have to make special efforts. Psychological experience in stepfamilies is very different from that in nuclear families of first marriages. The social bonds within the stepfamily are far more numerous and complicated. To build identifications between stepparents and stepchildren takes time and patience. Yet millions of Americans are succeeding at it. It will help them and the rest of us if everybody clearly understands the challenge.

All stepfamilies are built on loss. No matter how much joy and happiness stepfamilies bring—and they can bring a lot—the only people in them who have not been through the sadness of death or divorce are any previously unmarried spouses. Emily and John Visher, in *Step-Families* (1979), discuss this sympathetically. Remarried husbands and wives have suffered the loss of a relationship and perhaps the loss of their "dream." Children, when their parents divorce, not only have to adjust to a new relationship with each parent, but their identification as a part of their parents as a unit has been mangled.

Most of the adult members of stepfamilies and all of the children are "starting over" after some sort of catastrophe. Most of the children, on the other hand, are not so much starting over themselves as they are being dragged into their parents' new beginnings. A few of them are eager for the new marriage, and others accept it. But for many, the parents' starting over at remarriage marks a rift in their families starker than the divorce itself. It assures them that the split between their parents won't be healed. This loss is final.

The children's loss at the time of divorce was complicated because their parents, psychologically busy with their own adjustments, may have had little empathy with the mourning of the children. Not only was the child's development knocked temporarily off course, but the parents' capacity to parent may have been directly affected. Now, at remarriage, this is likely to happen again: the parent is caught up in his or her own starting over and may have neither the time nor the skill to empathize with the children.

At the time of a parent's remarriage, the children suffer a double blow. First, their parent is now part of a strange new unit with somebody who is an outsider to their old unit. Even more painful, they feel themselves outsiders to the new unit, and their new stepparent almost surely also considers them outsiders. There are two groups—indeed, two families—and the pivotal person in both of them is the natural parent.

To give some idea of the complexity of the stepfamily, let's start with an analysis of the role structure of the relatively simple nuclear family. The nuclear family can contain a maximum of eight roles. It has (1) a husband and (2) a wife, who as parents are (3) a mother and (4) a father. It can have (5) a son and (6) a daughter, who in reference to one another are (7) brother and (8) sister. Obviously, everybody in the nuclear family plays two roles. All the roles (except the husband and wife) can be repeated and played opposite several different individuals—and parents may play their roles differently with each child, and sisters and brothers may also be different with one sibling than with another.

The system of the nuclear family emerges because these eight roles can be arranged into eight possible dyadic relationships: husband-wife, father-son, mother-son, father-daughter, mother-daughter, brother-brother, sister-sister, and brother-sister. In order for all of the dyads to be present, the family has to have two or more sons and two or more daughters. In other cultures or languages, the number of relationships may come out differently. For example, some Native American languages have a single term for siblings of same sex and another for siblings of opposite sex. In that case, the language recognizes only two sibling relationships, which reduces the total number of dyads to seven. Some African languages have single words for a father–child and mother–child relationship instead of separating the children by sexes, thereby also reducing the number of relationships. But no matter what language or culture, the nuclear family is relatively simple.

When a parent dies or when one of the living parents moves out of the household, there are (in English) only five relationships in the remaining one-parent household. Such a household is understaffed. There are also three relationships external to the disjoined family—co-parents and the other two parent-child relationships. In a binuclear family, there are two households, each of which contains five relationships, with only the ex-husband–ex-wife co-parenting relationship outside.

The first trap for the stepfamily springs when parents remarry: they may think they are entering a family like the nuclear family and may even call it a "reconstituted" family. If the original nuclear families were both broken by death, there may indeed be an illusion of "reconstitution" when the surviving parents remarry. We can call this sort of stepfamily a simple stepfamily. It is simple not in the sense of its internal construction— you add four stepparent relationships, three half-sibling relationships, and three stepsibling relationships, making as many as eighteen possible relationships instead of the nuclear family's classic eight. Rather, it is simple because there is only one set of living co-parents. Simple stepfamilies stand alone as a nuclear family does, unencumbered by the demands or the images of surviving natural parents outside the household. Even here, the new and the old grandparents, the aunts and uncles and the new cousins make a more complex mix than can ever be found in a nuclear family, not only because there are more people, but because the source and nature of the relationships are different.

Stepfamilies that are built after divorce are more complex in their structure and *far* more complex emotionally. In families of divorce, as in nuclear families, there are eight dyads. The husband-wife relationship appears to be absent, but in fact it has been redefined into a co-parenting relationship between ex-husband and ex-wife. So the family of divorce actually retains the structure of the nuclear families; it is the *household* organization that has changed.

Then, when divorced parents each remarry a new spouse who already has children, and at least one of the new couples has a new baby, a really complicated structure emerges. The two interlocked households in a binuclear family have not disappeared, but something has been added. Each household may have become a stepfamily household, each with its 18 relationships (only the full-sibling relationships count in both). In addition you have three new outside relationships. The original co-parental relationship is the prime outside relationship. But add to it the relation between a woman's husband and her ex-husband and that of a man's wife and his ex-wife, and the relationship between the former spouses of the remarried couple. This last relationship can be a stabilizing factor, especially if, as sometimes happens, the new spouses can communicate with one another better than the former couple can. (These outside relationships participate in the household only at one remove.) That makes a total of 22 types of possible relationships involved in the stepfamily structure, some of them repeated several times.

From the children's point of view, they now seem to be members of two stepfamilies while they remain members of one binuclear family. It is structurally complex, and emotionally it can be much more difficult than adjusting to Dad's house and Mom's house. Children of a binuclear family are still, as they were before the remarriage, regular participants in two households, forming a link between them. But the two households of a binuclear family are now submerged in the new stepfamilies. The original co-parents, each remarried and living in a different stepfamily household, must still make decisions about the children and communicate about their movements. But now they must do it in a context in which the new spouses may see that original co-parenting relationship as a threat.

Ruth Roosevelt and Jeanette Lofas, in their 1976 how-to book called *Living in Step,* point out that new stepparents may have difficulty because they don't always come first with their new spouses. "If [a stepmother] feels that her husband's chief loyalty is to his children, she may do anything to come first with him—including trying to turn him against his children." To succeed, stepparents must accept from the start that their new mates already have families, and lower their expectations accordingly, adjusting themselves to the situation. If they saw this reality for what it was, some prospective new spouses might decide that the marriage wasn't worth it. The parent can ease the situation by making sure that his or her emotional separation from the former spouse as spouse is really complete, and by assuring the new spouse that his or her love for the children does not mean that the new spouse is unloved.

From the child's point of view, the new spouse is an intruder. Often, before the new marriage, children got along with prospective stepparents—when they could consider them as guests. It was "Mom's house," not "his house." It was "Dad's house," not "her house." After remarriage, ways of doing things in the two households may become even more different from one another. Wives and husbands usually cook to please each other; and the children are told to eat what is put before them. New couples create new routines—the system is at work again, and the children may not like what it produces. The expectations and standards of behavior set for the child change.

What studies there are indicate that children can adjust if the two natural parents allow the children to work out their own relationships not only with the other parent but with the stepparent, on terms worked out by that parent or stepparent and the child. Major difficulties are likely to arise only when one parent or stepparent criticizes the child's other parent and the way his or her household is run. The child, in part as a weapon, will almost surely compare the houses to the disadvantage of whichever one he or she happens to be in at the time. A parent's hostility to the ex can now be aimed at the ex's new spouse, opening up new kinds of trouble. All the things you didn't say before may now be said—about the new stepparent. There is a cultural norm that you don't run down the children's other parent, but nothing that says you can't run down the children's stepparent.

As a result of all these complex households, step-families (each of which includes segments of a binuclear household) form a sort of chain, what I some years ago called "divorce chains":

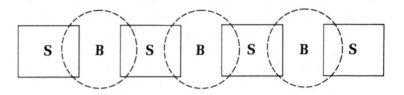

S = stepfamily   **B** = binuclear family

The way to deal with it is to keep straight in your mind which family is functioning at which time. A remarried man is tied to his ex for binuclear family purposes and to his wife for stepfamily purposes. By the same token his ex-wife is tied to her present husband for stepfamily purposes. It is easy to say that; it may be difficult to do it if unresolved emotions intrude.

Another way of looking at the stepfamily household makes it possible to understand its differences from another point of view: it contains in-laws. A mother-in-law in the house is likely in Western cultures to create strain; she is the butt of countless bad jokes. But step-children and stepparents are just as much in-laws as are parents-in-law. They are relatives by marriage, this time in the younger generation instead of the older generation. This in-law status is not a metaphor; two hundred years ago stepparents were called parents-in-law. There is one important difference, however. We can say that a mother-in-law lives in her children's house, but step-children are not guests. To a child, a parent's house is "my house." When children are turned into guests they instantly and correctly feel that they have been rejected.

Over and over people try to make a stepfamily household work just like a nuclear family household. As we
can see, that is a guarantee that it won't work at all. The
most important thing for you as a stepparent to remember is that your stepchild is not your child. He or she is a
child you may be able to learn to love, and who may be
able to learn to love you. Difficulties arise because stepparents have ideas about the way things are going to be,
and so do stepchildren. We are back to the old unconscious deal that accompanies the conscious contract.
Those ideas almost never work out in fact because the
family system results from the intertwining of those
ideas, played off on one another. A frequent difficulty is
that stepparents think they ought to love their stepchildren, and they don't, especially at first. Some kids
have exactly the opposite problem: they are supposed to
hate their stepparent (they know the myths too), and
often it turns out they don't but are reluctant to admit it.

Stepchildren have to learn not to confuse their stepparents with their real parents. That is not hard in one
sense, but it is hard to accept that both have a place, a
different place. Stepmothers have it easier if the child's
natural mother is being a good mother so that there is no
possibility of the two being in competition in the child's
perception. If—even especially if—the natural mother is
not doing her mothering well, the child is likely to stick
up for her and to resent even the stepmother who does it
better. Kids must be taught to realize that a stepparent
won't replace a parent, but may nevertheless become
very important in their lives.

The children, too, have to deal with the outside relationships. In every stepfamily household (as in the
binuclear household that is a part of it) the noncustodial
parent is a built-in joker. The external parent can play
havoc with the planning and activities of the new stepfamily, just as he or she can in the binuclear family.
Comparatively few external parents intentionally make
things rough. But children can try to use the outside

relationships for their own—sometimes disruptive—purposes.

The psychological maturation of a remarriage is very different from the trajectory of growth for a first marriage we examined in Chapter 7. The spouses are older when the second marriage is undertaken. But more important, the stages of psychological growth in a second marriage come in a different order and with different intensities. New identifications are to be built on the ruins of old identifications, and if you are still involved in a co-parenting league with a former spouse, identifications must be built so that one league does not destroy the other.

In a first marriage, we will remember, each partner finds in the other some aspects of her or his own ego ideal that have been repressed. So is it in a second marriage except that the process may come later in the relationship. When the relationship becomes sexual, an accommodation of the two ids takes place. So does an accommodation of the two super-egos. Each person takes into account the feelings, demands, and values of the other as well as of the self. That may happen much earlier in the relationship the second time around.

The next phase of growth of the relationship also occurs in remarriages—identification of spouses, when each perceives the other as not only an extension of self, but also as a criterion for judgment by third parties. The separation from the first spouse may also continue to be an important dimension of the self. That is, "I think the world thinks of me as the person who separated from my first spouse and took up with my second spouse."

The identifications become more numerous and complex in regard to children. In the nuclear family of a first marriage, each parent identifies with the children as they are born. You already see yourself in the child and the child in you, and you know that you and the child fit together. That also means that you almost automatically identify the child's other parent with your own parent of opposite sex. The remarrying parent comes into the relationship in a context in which all these old identifications are intact.

We have now arrived at the psychological heartland of divorce and remarriage. What happens to the old identifications when a marriage ends? The psychological work commonly called mourning includes adjusting these identifications to the new reality and may take many years. In the meantime what happens to the remnants of those old identifications when new identifications are being built with new spouses?

The vicissitudes of these identifications have never been adequately studied. Dreams could tell us a lot about this psychological process, but as far as I can find, no study of the dreams of people undergoing divorce has ever been published. Those few divorced people I know who can remember their dreams report that the qualities of their old spouses and their new partners get all mixed up in dream characters. Even years after remarriage, people still dream of their former spouses. It seems that you can't shed a spouse psychologically as readily as you can legally.

So remarriage and the stepfamily are built not only on loss, but inescapably also on foundations of identification from the past. First, you already have an identification with each one of your children. Second, you already have an identification (now much altered) with your ex-spouse. But it is the next identification—or lack of it—that is the major trap in the stepfamily: you almost certainly have no identification at all with the children of your new spouse. Identification with children, and of spouses with one another because of the children, are the psychological core of a nuclear, disjoined, or binuclear family. In a stepfamily, that identification must be slowly and more consciously built.

The identifications are equally complex for the children of a remarried parent. First, each child experiences each natural parent individually and experiences the league of the parents as "my parents." Most children assume an identification between their parents as an unstated premise of themselves. After the divorce, children have to adjust these identifications to a degree. The identification with each parent remains (even if the child ends up disliking one or both), but the identification with the couple, the league, has to change. Children must also reevaluate their identifications with siblings. The sibling bond may be strengthened or weakened, depending on the child's reaction first to any new leagues between single parent and child, and then to the new league between parent and stepparent.

The children's new identifications with stepparents may be difficult, particularly if they feel the new identifications to be in conflict or at odds with the parental identifications that are so much a part of their personalities. Identifying with the stepparent takes time. The job is to separate mother from stepmother, father from stepfather, and then to maintain two identifications without confusing them. I once interviewed a college student who told me that everything about himself that he liked came from his stepfather, while everything about himself that he didn't like he got from his father. Obviously, he had not yet figured out exactly who he was.

Identifying with your mother as your father's wife is somewhat different from identifying with your mother as some stranger's wife. If a child struggles with identifications with the father and the stepfather, the identification with the mother will certainly feel some reverberations. In addition, the parent's new identification in remarriage may actually work some surface personality change, which may be disturbing to the children. Finally, a child's identifications in the stepfamily are closely associated with the processes of psychological growth at various ages. Unfortunately, we don't yet know enough about all this because psychiatrists and therapists have not looked at it as a general phenomenon, separate from individual cases. If all this psychological work is done effectively, the person who has achieved it has many more identifications and an expanded self. Simplicity and straightforwardness may be lost, but the gain is a greater sophistication. The findings of social science since the 1950s have been that the adjustment of stepchildren to school and peers and family households is as good as the adjustment of natural children.

Ellen Galinsky in her book *Between Generations: The Six Stages of Parenthood*, examined nuclear families, disjoined families, binuclear families, and stepfamilies (although she did not mention the distinctions) and came up with a model of parenting that can be adapted as a guide to stepparenting. In her scheme, the stages of parenting in any kind of family are determined by the development of the child. At every stage, parents have what Galinsky calls images of how they themselves and their children *should* develop and behave—very like what we have called the dream or the unconscious deal of people who get married. If reality coincides with the images, they feel pleasure; if not, they get depressed and angry.

Galinsky has divided parenthood into six stages: (1) image-making; (2) nurturing; (3) authority; (4) interpretive; (5) interdependent; and (6) departure. Parents, because of their identification with the children, are led through the six stages. If there are several children, they may be in several stages at once. As we saw earlier, the parent not only experiences being the parent but at the same time vicariously experiences being the child, remembering his or her own history.

The image-making stage in the nuclear family coincides with the pregnancy. For stepfamilies, this phase occurs during the courtship and "stepping in" of the stepparent. During the stepfamily's image-making stage, both the natural and new stepparent prepare for the changes that will occur in themselves and what they think their relationship will become. A new parental league is being forged. If a stepparent is to move into a one-parent household, then this new league between the adults is essential.

At this same time, the stepparent begins to pull together ideas about what kind of stepparent he or she will be. Natural parents think about how a stepparent will change their own parenting. The two of them create images—often unconscious—of how stepparenting will affect their relationship as spouses. They begin the processes of creating identifications among their new spouses, their old spouses, their own parents, the new stepchildren, and their own children.

Just as you are likely to make an unconscious contract when you get married, prospective stepparents often spin fantasies about what the stepchildren will do at the same time that they think about what they themselves are doing. If these images accord well with reality, they can be of immense help; if they don't, both the stepparent and the children are in for trouble. If the stepparent-to-be has considerable contact with the stepchildren-to-be, he or she may be able to get the images fairly well aligned with those of the children. But many stepparents do not see their own images clearly. A research project in the middle 1970s found that stepfathers did not rate themselves as highly as natural fathers did, but their wives and stepchildren rated them just as highly. There may be two reasons for that. One is that natural fathers have no need at this stage of parenting to think about how complicated being a father is, and they therefore assume that they are good at it. Stepfathers have thought about it far more and are not so sure. The other reason is that natural fathers do not hear much criticism from the outside world, no matter what they do. Stepfathers hear a lot, also no matter what they do.

Perhaps the hardest thing about creating an image of oneself as a stepparent is the negative folk-image, particularly of stepmothers. Yet, in spite of generations of successful and loving stepparents, there are no ready-made images for stepparents except the cruel stereotypes. Where does the idea come from that "stepmothers are cruel"? Like all myths and fairy tales, it has two sources: one historical and the other psychological. "The fact of the stepmother" is cruelty of fate, not that any particular stepmother need be cruel to perpetuate the folk tale. The only studies indicate that, taken as a group, stepmothers are no more cruel that natural mothers.

Many stepmothers have difficulty even pronouncing the word "stepmother," let alone so identifying themselves. And children know all those stories well—the culture builds into them negative images that must be overcome. The fact is that (with some exceptions, for there are cruel stepmothers just as there are cruel natural mothers) the cruelty of the stepmother is not in her person, but in the system. The less well the system is understood, the more cruel she is likely to look.

Parenthood enters the nurturing stage with the birth of a child in the nuclear family; it lasts until the child learns to say "no." The major parental task at that time is to cement an attachment to the infant and reconcile the differences between the real infant and the imagined child. If the child does not "live up to" the image, the parent has to redefine it. There may be a period of mourning for the image, even as it is successfully replaced. The easiest thing to do—and naive parents sometimes do it—is to assume that the child is bad because he or she does not live up to the parental image.

For stepparents, the nurturing stage has different rhythms to which the stepparent must adjust. It is far more difficult to pick up the rhythm of a 6-year-old or a 13-year-old than the rhythm of a newborn. Neither the stepparent nor the stepchild is likely to be ready for this sudden change. Moreover, a natural parent is a parent in his or her own right, while a stepparent is a parent by allowance from the natural parent. The natural parent can dictate the amount of authority and kind of discipline that the stepparent will apply to the children. The stepparent has no memories of the sweet infant to draw on when the older child behaves hatefully, and no God-given right to correct the child's behavior.

An identity problem may arise at this stage if the child resembles the absent natural parent, just as there is sometimes difficulty for natural parents if the child resembles a disliked relative. Such assessments of physical resemblance to other people often color attitudes to the child; in stepfamilies they may create serious problems.

When the child learns to say "no," parents enter the authority stage. The primary parental responsibilities are to keep the child out of danger while allowing some leeway for the child to explore the environment, and to instill the requirements of the parents and the society. A parent at this stage is a hate-object as well as a love-object. Some parents, and almost all stepparents, find it difficult to be hate-objects. But stepparents can be hate-objects without ever being love-objects at the same time. There may at those moments also be no ambivalence in the stepparent: when the child is hateful, it is hard to do much except hate back. The task of establishing authority is extremely diffuse in the stepfamily. It is important in this stage that the major task be to avoid battles of will. A study of stepfathers by Phyllis Stern suggests that authority is the gravest problem they face. At the heart of this matter is the question of who is the disciplinarian and under what circumstances. Who has to mind whom? What are the sanctions if they do not? It may take a lot of stepfamily conferences to get this all out in the open. Social scientists who have studied stepchildren find a correlation between their view of whether the stepparent loves them and whether the stepparent makes them behave. "He doesn't make me mind, therefore he doesn't love me." is their complaint. Just as difficult is the dictatorial stepparent who will not listen to the child's view. Often the wife/mother has an image of the stepfather's taking considerable authority, but she is not always prepared to relinquish any of her own authority to allow him to do so. And not dealing plainly and straightforwardly with the authority of the step-mother is probably an important factor in her evil reputation.

The interpretive stage of parenthood begins when the child starts school and continues until he or she reaches puberty. The child, at the end of this time, has absorbed the parents' view of society and the world. This stage, like any other, is triggered by the growth of the child, and the parent's task is to keep up. Galinsky makes an important point when she says that the way the parents interpret the world is not merely culture-bound—that is, imparts the standard cultural view—and not even merely family-bound; it is specific for each child. The presence of stepparents means that the child can pick up wider views, which is good if there is no serious conflict among the views.

A child may check out everything the stepparent says with the "real" parent, both the one in the same household and the one outside it. The child tallies the step-parent's evaluations with those of the natural parents, and is likely to opt for the natural parent's evaluation, creating still more strain in the stepparent relationship. This period can be traumatic if the stepparent needs the child's validation or gratitude. Parents never get thanked until, perhaps, years later. Neither do stepparents. The difference is that stepparents may expect it.

The interdependent stage begins at or shortly before the child's puberty. It has been said that stepparenting an adolescent is the most difficult of all, especially if the stepping-in occurs at that time. The identity of the teen-ager is formed, but it is likely to be tentative and insecure. The task of creating new kinds of ties while at the same time allowing and encouraging greater distance is difficult even in the nuclear family and is very touchy in the stepfamily. Stepparents—perhaps correctly—are likely to view this pulling away as a rejection of the stepfamily. If stepparents urge adolescents to get too closely involved with the stepfamily, they can expect resistance.

The sixth stage is the departure stage, when the children are actually in the process of leaving home. Natural parents all too often have an image of their relationship with one another as it was before children were born, thus building images of themselves that are seriously out of phase with reality. The comparable trap for stepparents is thinking that as soon as the kids leave, their relationship can begin to be what they wanted it to be all along.

In successful stepfamilies, the natural parent is the pivot. The husband-wife league must be absolutely tight, though not at the expense of weakening parent-child links or of threatening the league of the divorced parents in rearing their children. The parent is thus involved in two leagues—one with the present-spouse-stepparent and the other with the former-spouse-parent. The moment a natural parent sides with the child against a stepparent (or, indeed, vice versa) instead of supporting the other parent, even in disagreement, the child has a wedge to break open the new marriage. And children of all ages, even adult children, are likely to try. When the two co-parents allow the stepparent into the league, just a little, the job is probably easier for all concerned.

A tight and rewarding marital relationship can allow the parent and stepparent to deal with the difficulties of the children by understanding them, assuring the child that they know how he or she feels, and that with time and effort negative feelings will fade.

One interesting external dimension of stepfamilies occurs where the grandparents are concerned. Stepgrandparents and stepgrandchildren need help in working out a rewarding relationship with one another. Both need to be convinced that love will grow or else that it will not, but in no case can it be instantaneous. Grandparents often fear that they will lose their grandchildren when those grandchildren's parents get divorced. Occasionally they do, but not as often as they fear. And further difficulty between the parents and the grandparents may emerge when new stepgrandchildren suddenly arrive. Grandparents can be crude in the favoritism they show their natural grandchildren over their stepgrandchildren. It is "natural" feeling for "their own" and they don't even think about the fact that the stepgrandchildren may interpret it as a cruel exclusion. At remarriage, a child gets a new set of grandparents: a stepchild may have six or eight grandparents instead of the ordinary four. Some grandparents find that kind of sharing difficult. But when they can manage it, the children prosper.

One of three children in the next decade will experience the stepfamily. We must undertake far more research and give more help to the people who establish stepfamilies to make them work. A stepfamily can survive if people do not try to run a complex organization with the rules of simple organizations. Stepfamilies are different from nuclear families: they are more complicated, there are more people in them, and more traps. But for those stepfamilies who have worked out the details, they may be even more rewarding.

Part III

Toward a Well-family Industry

Toward a
Well-family Industry

In the next quarter century, we should put as much social creativity into developing a well-family industry as we have, during the last quarter century, put into the divorce industry. When you look back to the 1960s, you can see that we have achieved a lot. Although going through divorce is, and will no doubt remain, a miserable experience, the divorce procedure itself is far more honest; the legal dimensions of the break-up are far less messy, and support for divorced people and their families far greater.

We must now take the next step—creating a viable well-family industry. This requires knowing the answers to difficult questions such as, "What goals ought we to have for families?" or "What can a well-family industry do?" To find these answers, we need to know a number of things.

First, we have to do a better job of investigating observable behavior. A repeated complaint in this book has been the state of our knowledge about the family. There is an immense literature on the family, most of it superficial, unimaginative, and repetitious. Most of the studies are limited in scope and full of unexamined premises. Few of them examine the areas where our ignorance is greatest. We need fresh, unprejudiced observation that will allow us to question our ideas and confirm them if they are any good, rather than more tired questionnaires that address the same old issues.

Second, any well-family industry depends on clarification of the premises that underlie our social thought. There are two kinds of premises: those of which we are aware, and those we do not know we hold. In any thinking about social matters, the most important premises, the ones that determine the questions we ask and hence the answers we get, are likely to be outside our awareness.

Lurking premises about the family abound. For parents, for example, they are the images of what the child is that we examined in Chapter 11. For an individual's self-perception, the lurking premises take the form of the dream of what he or she will become and what a successful life will be like. For a newly marrying couple, the unconscious contract is a whole system of lurking premises.

As long as the premises only lurk, scientists or spouses or ordinary people keep expecting the outside world to look like the picture in their minds. When it doesn't, they are likely to pretend it does or knock themselves out trying to make things match, without questioning whether they can or should. We have to be clear about what we believe about the family, so that we can distinguish beliefs from reality.

Finally, to plan for a well-family industry we must understand what Daniel Yankelovich has called the plate tectonics of society. In geology, tectonics are the deformations of the Earth's crust—the mountains, plateaus, faults, ocean ridges, rigid parts that move slowly in juxtaposition to one another. When the plates collide or slip past or over one another, mountains may rise, earthquakes occur, volcanoes erupt.

The plate tectonics of society concern fundamental changes in social institutions, specifically when change in one institution brings about dislocation in another quite different one. Social forms like the family are part of a larger system, and until we understand that, we cannot fully understand the constituent institutions. The slow grinding of the social tectonics and the power of the lurking premises combined to keep us from seeing until recently what was happening to the family. The family has not gone to the dogs; rather, its type has been changing. We may never know all of the forces that can change our families, but we can be better prepared by knowing that society is a system and that everything is connected, whether or not the connection is obvious.

We have at least to entertain the idea that a well-family industry already exists but that we cannot yet see it. Family service agencies often provide magnificent service (although too often only after serious difficulties have set in). Family therapy, developed in the 1950s, has come almost as far since 1970 as has the divorce industry. Today, there are far more family therapists, far better trained. Now many clergymen and women are trained not only in theology and public speaking but also in human relations, so that churches can give much more than admonitions and sympathy.

A genuine and wide-based commitment to the family is one of the greatest needs. Families should have a place on the social agendas of lawmakers, activists, and the general public. Unless the other institutions of society intensify their concern for and interaction with the family, the pressures of the social plate tectonics that shape the family will go unheeded. If we are to plan a well-family industry, we must know what other institutions are consciously or unconsciously doing to the family.

For example, if so many mothers are working, what are the attitudes of business and industry to the family? A few employers have begun to, or been forced to, take consideration of the family—supporting variable hours (flextime), maternity leaves, paternity leaves, and day-care centers. However, in all of New York City not a single employer yet offers on-site day care for employees' children. There is also less random transferring of executives and workers to new communities than there was two or three decades ago, which means less wear and tear on families. Because the law demands it, most employers today provide health benefits and retirement. Nevertheless, few of them have adopted a consistent family policy or gone beyond a crude general statement that they "care" about families. At least as much time is lost in industry through family problems as through alcoholism or illness (although, since it is largely the time of lower-paid women, many employers deem it less important).

Even the schools are in a new position vis-à-vis the family. They have, in recent decades, been asked to provide all-day childcare while the parents work. At the same time, the association between family and school is changing. Before World War II, the school was an integral part of a community. Today the community served by a school is seven or eight times larger than it was only a few decades ago. Because the connection between community and the schools has changed, the people who live in the geographical area served by the school (no longer a community in the same sense) vote to provide less money to the schools.

The military services are, on some levels, aware that they interlink with families. They provide medical service and commissary prices to the families of servicemen and women. The Navy, for example, is concerned because service at sea is so hard on family life that some wives pressure their husbands not to reenlist. But naval research on the family centers as much on how to get the wives to stop badgering their husbands as on how to improve the family life of sailors. Except during depressions, the services have trouble attracting enough able recruits to staff a professional army, and sometimes they blame "the family" for not providing the kind of sons and daughters they can use. This is an example of a far more general phenomenon—the family is blamed for not doing everything the other institutions of society define as its province.

Neighborhoods are families in a way. However, neighborhood and community no longer overlap; people of common interest usually no longer live in the same neighborhoods. Children's play groups and the school may now be the only social groups that hold the remnants of a neighborhood together. Social tectonics have been at work again.

The place of government policy in family matters is more complicated. Few Americans want the government to set our family policy. Yet when the legislative branch overlooks the impact of new laws on the family—from labor law to Social Security and welfare law—one wishes that politicians realized that almost everything they do connects with families, and that they may interfere in families every time they pass a law in some other area of life.

Every step that the government makes to improve family life is based on somebody's (probably unconscious) premises and definition of the family. The welfare laws that unwittingly run fathers, or substitute fathers, out of homes are only the most notorious example.

We need systematically to assess the impact that all laws, new and old, have on families. Lawmakers, judges, and social scientists could compile a set of thoughtful principles (not just yesteryear's platitudes) to judge them by.

When we begin the process of organizing a well-family industry, we should make our values about families very clear. I am going to state my own values here. I do not expect everybody to agree with them.

1. Marriage is *nobody's* business except that of the people who are involved in it. We have spent too many centuries trying to control marriage. The days when

233

marriages served political and economic functions as well as providing child-rearing and psychological intimacy are gone.

2. Parenthood is *everybody's* business. We have for too many centuries said that children are the chattels of their parents, and added that nobody else should interfere in parenting. If we have to control anything, we should control parenting in order to ensure that children have as good a shake as we can give them.

Right now we can begin the process of giving the children top priority when we adjust to divorce. We have to stop getting the co-parents divorced in a way that makes it impossible for them to cooperate even minimally after the decree. Until the law catches up, we could start by ritualizing divorce as a renewed pledge to the welfare of the children. Even for those who don't like ritual, a public statement is a good idea.

We should encourage good parent-child relationships, in whatever kind of family the child lives, and stop treating one-parent families or families of divorce as if in themselves they were abnormal. As long as we continue, by our individual decisions, to create a high divorce rate, they are anything but.

3. The success of the family is the responsibility of *everybody* in it, particularly the parents. No longer can we expect the wife and mother to take on the full weight of making a success of the family at the expense of her other interests and capacities.

Human beings have discovered fatherhood, but because the family is inextricably tied up with women (it is also tied up with men, but we perceive the connections differently), we must work out new ways of rearing the young now that women's cultural horizons are expanding. The definition of a male chauvinist might be someone who wants to force women back into a role of child-rearing, like the nonhuman mammals, merely because she is female. Feminists do not object to being parents. They object to being infracultural.

By principles of social tectonics, the nature of fatherhood is changing. Because paternity is cultural, ideas about it and the behavior of doing it can change very fast. The form of the traditional family was determined by a culturally accepted sexual division of tasks; that division has now changed and we have begun to give new meaning to paternity.

Therefore, the present fear for the future of the family really isn't about the family at all. It is about a particular form of family. And beyond that, it is about the positions of women and of men. Feminism subscribes to a form of family that does not imprison women; as Letty Cottin Pogrebin points out, the very words "the family" when it is "used prescriptively," can still "coerce people into roles" and can "transform nostalgia into votes" and "create a national ethos out of a myth of domestic bliss." The lurking premise for too many people who want to save the family is that it should be done with the lives of women.

4. The family is the responsibility of *all* the institutions of society. As long as the family is our primary institution for rearing the next generation, other institutions have responsibility for it as well.

Americans in the late twentieth century have been living with a contradiction. We have long operated on the old theological and legal premise that marriage is the cornerstone of the family. But we have lately come to accept the psychotherapist's premise that marriage should be rewarding and expanding. The first premise says that divorce is unequivocally and always bad; the second that, bad as it may be, it may also be essential to mature growth.

We should get our premises straight. The most important one for the future is that good families are the ones that make good children. The second that good parenthood, not merely a happy marriage, is the essence of a good family and of good society, no matter what form those families take.

A Bibliographic Essay: Some Writings About the Family

The longer an investigator has worked on a subject, the more difficult it is to know for sure where the ideas have come from. This short essay provides both a guide to the materials I have consciously used in writing this book and some additional works that have influenced me but are not directly cited.

The literature on the family is one of the largest in all of social science. It is also one of the worst. The primary reason is that social scientists are as subject to the prejudices of their time as anyone else. We have not been able to get much distance from the family or to rise far enough above our knee-jerk reactions.

This makes it urgent that we try harder than ever to view the family dispassionately and to be aware of the unstated assumptions we bring to any examination of it. The philosopher Alfred North Whitehead has said that if we want to make a contribution to any subject, the way to proceed is to question that premise longest left unquestioned. But since most of our premises are unconscious, the trick in Whitehead's admonition is to discover what they are. It has been my purpose to question several premises that we have managed to make overt, the most important of which is that we must control marriage if we are to affect the characteristics and quality of family life. I think that premise is demonstrably false, and that we still believe it only because we haven't examined it; the last 3,000 years of family history prove its falsity. So far as I have read about the family, I have looked for what has been said through the ages that allows us to question that premise.

Little has been written specifically on what I have in this book called the divorce industry. As far as I know, the phrase is mine—I began using it in 1980—but *The Journal of Divorce*, edited by Esther Oshiver Fisher, contains articles on many aspects of that industry. My material on matrimonial lawyers comes primarily from my own field inquiries, largely in California and Chicago. The number of people who helped was legion, but I want particularly to mention Kathryn Gehrels, Herma Hill Kay, and Ann Diamond of San Francisco, and Joseph DuCanto of Chicago, who for many years have been of immense help.

The plight of divorce judges in the early 1960s was evident as I interviewed them, both in San Francisco, San Mateo, and Santa Clara counties of California, and in Chicago in 1963 and again in 1980 and 1981. I talked to a number of judges, but want especially to thank Judge Donald King of San Francisco and Judge Charles Fleck of Chicago for their forthrightness and insight. Most judges, of course, did not write about their frustration. The article by the one who did, Judge C. Pfeiffer Trowbridge, appeared in *The Florida Bar Journal*, vol. 30, no. 10 (November, 1963), pp. 1023–29. It seems in questionable taste today, and may even have been at the time, but it reflects the way that many judges were talking in the early 1960s.

The history of the family as a serious pursuit among historians is recent. The "classics" are now old: *the* classic is the magnum opus of the Finnish anthropologist, Edward Westermarck, *The History of Human Marriage*. I use the fifth edition (some printings dated 1922, and some 1925) because it was the last. Westermarck was astonishingly thorough and admirably cross-cultural, but his book reflects the premises of his age, and his anthropology has long since been outmoded. Therefore, the book has to be read with historians' eyes: one eye on the data, the other on the ideology behind them. Since Westermarck there have been no large-scale studies of the family across cultures and histories—indeed, such an attempt would probably no longer be possible or even useful.

The standard history of marriage in the United States is by Arthur Wallace Calhoun, *A Social History of the American Family,* originally published in 1917 (the edition I use is New York: Barnes and Noble, 1975). Because it is so steeped in the theological cant of its day, and his premises kept his inquiring mind in such strict bondage, it is almost unreadable today as anything other than a document about the moral pressures and premises of the early part of the twentieth century.

Recently a number of historical studies of the family in specific places and times have appeared. Among the best is Lawrence Stone's *The Family, Sex and Marriage in England, 1500-1800* (New York: Harper & Row, 1978). Stone's mastery not only of the sources for his period, but of the social science of families, is impressive. Two other specialized histories are William L. O'Neill's *Divorce in the Progressive Era* (New Haven: Yale University Press, 1967) and Elaine Tyler May's *Great Expectations: Marriage and Divorce in Post-Victorian America* (Chicago: University of Chicago Press, 1980). May examined court records of 500 case histories in Los Angeles County, California, in the 1880s, and another 500 from the 1920s, with a sort of control group from the conservative state of New Jersey—225 cases in the 1920s. It is an admirable piece of historical social science. Nevertheless, in spite of such historical monographs, there is no single source to which one can go to read anything like a modern exhaustive history of the family.

The best thing I have found on the very early history of marriage and divorce is Karl M. Rodman's "A Brief History of Marriage and Divorce," *Oregon Law Review*, vol. 23 (1944), pp. 249–63. His review of Greek and Roman practices and of Hebrew ideas and institutions is an effective summary; written primarily for lawyers, it nevertheless covers all the basics. Unfortunately, its detail stops at the beginning of the modern period. I have accepted Rodman's dates for separating the periods of the history of marriage and divorce in the West. An interesting view—hardly history, hardly social science, and indeed, hardly even jurisprudence, but instructive nevertheless—is presented by Karl Llewellyn in "Behind the Law of Divorce," *Columbia Law Review*, vols. 32 (1932) and 33 (1933).

Books on divorce in any age tend to be exercises in special pleading. One of the best early ones is J. P. Lichtenberger, *Divorce, A Social Interpretation* (New York: Whittlesey House, 1931). Scholarly histories of divorce are rare: the best is Nelson Manfred Blake's *The Road to Reno* (New York: Macmillan, 1962). I have leaned heavily on it. Unfortunately, Blake did not update it in the 1970s, when so much changed.

One of the finest legal thinkers about marriage and divorce was the late Max Rheinstein. He trained an immense number of those teaching and practicing today. Rheinstein perceptively compared the divorce law and practice of many lands in *Marriage Stability, Divorce and the Law* (Chicago: University of Chicago Press, 1972). Much of the information about California divorce during the 1960s and after comes from Rheinstein. However, I was myself a minor participant in parts of the California reform efforts and some of the material comes from my notes and from my recollections.

The quotation from Bertrand Russell in Chapter 2 is from *Marriage and Morals* (London: Allen and Unwin, 1929), a thoughtful "liberal" view of the difficulties with divorce in England and the United States in the 1920s.

Maxine Virtue's *Family Cases in Court* (Durham, N.C.: Duke University Press, 1956) is the report of a study done by the Commission on Uniform State Laws in one of its early attempts to remodel or at least rationalize divorce laws. It is useful in documenting what divorce was like in the 1940s and 1950s.

There are many valuable family books by feminists in recent years. I have cited Riane Tennenhaus Eisler, *Dissolution: No-Fault Divorce, Marriage and the Future of Women* (New York: McGraw-Hill, 1977) and Letty Cottin Pogrebin, *Family Politics: Love and Power on the Intimate Frontier* (New York: McGraw-Hill, 1983).

Ivan F. Nye wrote an influential article, "Child Adjustment in Broken and in Unhappy, Unbroken Homes," *Marriage and Family Living*, vol. 19 (1957), pp. 356–66.

Although Mormons have told me that they disapprove of the book, nevertheless, in my opinion the most balanced treatment of Mormon polygyny is Kimball Young's *Isn't One Wife Enough?* (New York: Henry Holt, 1954). Young was a social psychologist who taught for years in the sociology departments first at the University of Wisconsin, then at Northwestern. He was himself an apostate Mormon, though his name shows his lineage to be impeccable. Young remembered his grandfather Brigham Young as an old man—his reminiscences were valuable, and some of his stories uproarious. I have also discussed the nature of Mormon family life with sociologist Carlfred Broderick and am grateful for his views and analysis. Most of the literature on Mormon polygyny—and, I believe, all of the literature contemporary with its occurrence—is special pleading. I early gave up trying to pursue this literature thoroughly because to do it justice would have taken me far afield and contributed little to my understanding the institution. Those scholars who might claim that I have depended too fully on Kimball Young, either his book or his conversation, may be right.

Interestingly, there are few books comparing several instances of polygyny, mainly, I think, because it is fairly easy to understand. Remi Clignet's *Many Wives, Many Powers: Authority and Power in Polygynous Families* (Evanston: Northwestern University Press, 1970) is helpful, as is the chapter called "African Families" in my own *Africa and Africans* (New York: Natural History Press, 1964).

Polyandry, on the other hand, is so rare and so outré that there are good books about it. The classic early study of polyandry was W. H. R. Rivers' *The Toda* (London: Macmillan, 1906). Prince Peter of Greece and Denmark, an anthropologist who spent years studying polyandry, wrote many articles, summarized in a book, *A Study of Polyandry* (The Hague: Mouton, 1963), which may tell you, at the very least, all you ever wanted to know about the subject. It does not, however, emphasize the relationship between polyandry and paternity that I have stressed.

All of us are deeply indebted to Kathleen Gough for her perceptive field research among the Nayar of south India, and her explication of their marriage system. The most relevant article in the current context is "The Nayars and the Definition of Marriage," *Journal of the Royal Anthropological Institute*, vol. 89 (1959), pp. 23–24. Anyone claiming to be thoroughly conversant about the family must know David Schneider and Kathleen Gough, *Matrilineal Kinship* (Berkeley: University of California Press, 1961).

The reference to Alice Balint's vignette about the "horrid dog" is from her article, "Identification," *International Journal of Psycho-Analysis*, vol. 24 (1943), pp. 97–107.

Abigail Trafford's *Crazy Time* (New York: Harper &

Row, 1983) is an extraordinarily good account by a journalist of the period immediately following the break-up of a marriage. Another useful journalist's book (but not as good as Trafford's) is Elizabeth Cauhape's *Fresh Starts* (New York: Basic Books, 1983).

Morton Hunt is among the finest of journalists dealing with social science topics. His two books on divorce are important because they cover several areas of the experience not otherwise documented. It is difficult to believe today, but it is true, that almost nothing was generally known about the subculture of divorce at the time that Hunt published *The World of the Formerly Married* (New York: McGraw-Hill, 1966). Not quite ten years later, he and Bernice Hunt wrote *The Divorce Experience* (New York: McGraw-Hill, 1977).

Therapists' books are a lot like journalists' books, but the information in them is gathered in different ways. Journalists talk to all sorts of people, and the results are as good as their sources, their ears, and their background knowledge. Therapists' books, on the other hand, are based on information and insights from their patients—though, again, the ultimate quality depends on their background knowledge. Both are likely to be associated with personal experience, and to verge on the how-to book. One such combination of therapist's book and how-to-do-it, which will stand for many, is Mel Krantzler's influential and helpful *Creative Divorce* (New York: M. Evans, 1973).

My own *Divorce and After* (New York: Doubleday, 1970) grew out of an anthropological field research problem. I had been invited to spend the academic year 1963–64 at the Center for Advanced Study in the Behavioral Sciences at Stanford. That year, the founding Director, Dr. Ralph Tyler, had just got word from the Ford Foundation that the current five-year grant would be the last. Dr. Tyler suggested to the incoming fellows that if even half of us could bring our own salaries, he would have almost ten years instead of only five to build endowment for the Center. I had long been interested in what in those days was called social disorganization, as well as in the family, particularly the African family. Putting those two together spells divorce, so I applied for and received a grant to study divorce in crosscultural perspective from the National Institute of Mental Health. Soon after I began the study I discovered that the literature on the subject was uninformative. Without intending to, I found myself in the field.

After I published *Divorce and After,* I thought my studies of divorce were over. But in 1980, Lenore Weitzman of Stanford University told me that as far as she could determine, my case histories of divorce before the change of the California law in 1970 were unique. That set me to thinking, and as a result, with a Guggenheim fellowship, I replicated the original study in 1980–81.

Other publications of mine that form a background to the material in this book are "Before Divorce: Some Comments about Alienation in Marriage," in *Cultural Illness and Health; Essays in Human Adaptation,* Laura Nader and Thomas W. Maretzki, eds. [Anthropological Studies no. 9, David H. Maybury-Lewis, ed. (Washington, D.C.: American Anthropological Association, 1973)], and "Marriage and Divorce" in *Comprehensive Textbook in Psychiatry,* 3rd ed., Harold I. Kaplan, Alfred M. Freedman, and Benjamin J. Sadock, eds. (Baltimore: Williams and Wilkins, 1980), about boundaries and the crisis structure in marriages that end in divorce.

Paul Gebhard's "Postmarital Coitus among Widows and Divorcees" (in my *Divorce and After*) is the Kinsey Institute study about female orgasm after divorce or widowhood.

The most important articles on children and divorce by Mavis Hetherington and her co-workers are "Effects of father absence on personality development in adolescent daughters," *Developmental Psychology,* vol. 7 (1972), pp. 313–26, and "Girls without Fathers," *Psychology Today,* vol. 6, no. 2 (1972), pp. 47–52. With

Martha Cox and Roger Cox, she wrote "Divorced Fathers," *The Family Coordinator,* vol. 25, no. 4 (1976), pp. 417–28, and "The Aftermath of Divorce," in *Mother-child, Father-child Relations,* J. H. Stevens, Jr., and Marilyn Matthews, eds. (Washington, D.C.: NAEYC, 1977). Most important, Hetherington herself wrote "Divorce: A Child's Perspective," *American Psychologist,* vol. 23 (1979), pp. 851–58.

As of this writing, far and away the best book on the impact of divorce on children is by Judith Wallerstein and Joan Berlin Kelly, *Surviving the Breakup* (New York: Basic Books, 1980). During the course of my research, I also had several talks with Kelly, who was most helpful in filling in details.

Parts of the information about children of divorce in Chapter 5 derive from conversations held over the years with university students whose parents had been or were being divorced. Except for one group of about 20 that I sought out in the middle 1960s, the others came to me because they knew that I had studied the topic. I did not study these young people in any methodical way, but what they told me fits with both the Hetherington and the Wallerstein and Kelly accounts.

Journalist Linda Bird Francke wrote a long feature for *Newsweek* (February 11, 1980) called "Children of Divorce" that she expanded into *Growing Up Divorced* (New York: Simon & Schuster, 1983). The social attitudes toward children that result from the conditions of life in the United States since 1960, including the frequency of parental divorce, is the subject of Marie Winn's *Children Without Childhood* (New York: Pantheon Books, 1983), and Neil Postman's *The Disappearance of Childhood* (New York: Delacorte Press, 1982). These books raise the possibility that we are indeed in the midst of a major shift in our ideas about children that is comparable to the one detailed by Philippe Ariès in *Centuries of Childhood* (New York: Vintage, 1962).

Ideas about successful divorce were late in coming.

In 1948 the psychoanalyst Edmund Bergler reported in *Divorce Won't Help* (New York: Harper & Row) that divorce never solves any problems because divorce is an act of neurosis. Today, almost nobody holds such a view. Later, in 1956, William J. Goode more or less began modern systematic sociological study of divorce in a book that is still well worth reading, *After Divorce* (Glencoe, Ill.: Free Press). In the years since then, a great deal of the most insightful thinking about divorce bears the name of Jessie Bernard. As early as 1942, she published *American Family Behavior* (New York: Harper & Row). Then she gave us *Remarriage: A Study of Marriage* (New York: Dryden Press, 1956). After a series of articles and other books came *The Future of Marriage* (New York: World, 1972). The sociological study of the American family would be pallid indeed were it not for the works of Jessie Bernard.

The basic source on the psychological stages of growth of adults in families is Therese Benedek's brilliant article "The Emotional Structure of the Family," in Ruth Nanda Anshen's *The Family: Its Function and Destiny*, 2d ed. (Harper & Row, 1959). Benedek was that rare creature, a psychoanalyst who fully understood the difference between culture and psyche, where they were alike and where they parted company. She was one of the first psychoanalysts to delve deeply into the psyches of women and to show their differences from those of men, whom most of the theory described. Her work on the relation between dreams and the menstrual cycle still stands alone. Benedek's articles have been collected as *Psychoanalytic Investigations* (New York: Quadrangle, 1973).

The quotation from Bruno Bettelheim in Chapter 7 is from *The Informed Heart: Autonomy in a Mass Age* (Glencoe, Ill.: Free Press, 1960).

There are a number of books on one-parent families, most of them out of date. Indeed, almost everything before 1975 (and some things since) are out of date because our knowledge of and attitudes about the subject have changed so much in the last decade. The best source I have found is Robert Weiss, *Going It Alone* (New York: Basic Books, 1979). His *Marital Separation* (New York: Basic Books, 1975), and "The Emotional Impact of Marital Separation," *Journal of Social Issues,* vol. 32 (1978), pp. 135–45, are also helpful.

The immense literature on the postdivorce family, most of it about disjoined families, falls into three sorts. There are a few studies by social scientists, such as the work of psychologist Mavis Hetherington at the University of Virginia, cited above, and Andrew Cherlin's *Marriage, Divorce, Remarriage: Changing Patterns in the Postwar United States* (Cambridge: Harvard University Press, 1981), which focuses on demography.

Another important researcher is sociologist Frank Furstenberg of the University of Pennsylvania who, with a series of partners, has put out many articles of great interest. Among the most useful are "Recycling the Family: Perspectives for Researching a Neglected Family Form," *Marriage and Family Review,* vol. 2 (1979), pp. 12–22, "Reflections on Remarriage: Introduction to Special Issue on Remarriage," *Journal of Family Issues,* vol. 1 (1980), and "Conjugal Succession: Reentering Marriage after Divorce," in P. B. Baltes and O. G. Brim, eds., *Life Span Development and Behavior,* vol. 4 (New York: Academic Press, 1982).

Social worker Constance Ahrons, now at the University of Wisconsin, is one of our most creative thinkers and researchers on problems of the postdivorce family. Here I should cite "The Binuclear Family," *Alternative Lifestyles,* vol. 2, no. 4 (1979), pp. 499–515, and "Divorce: A Crisis of Family Transition and Change," *Family Relations,* vol. 29 (1980). Ahrons is just completing a five-year longitudinal study of communication in the postdivorce family; her early results indicate that this work will be of signal importance in our continuing revaluation of families.

Jean Goldsmith of the Center for Family Studies of Northwestern University's Psychiatry Department has consistently been one of the most important contributors to our understanding of the family as a system. Here I draw special attention to her excellent chapter, "The Postdivorce Family System," in *Normal Family Processes*, Froma Walsh, ed. (New York: Guilford Press, 1982). Virginia Satir's *Conjoint Family Therapy* (Palo Alto, Calif.: Science and Behavior Books, 1963) is a classic that contains a fine outline of what we knew about families in those days. Her *Peoplemaking* (Palo Alto, Calif.: Science and Behavior Books, 1972) is a more popular book that can be read with great profit.

Susan Steinman of the San Francisco Jewish Family Services was one of the first to carry out research in the area of the binuclear family. "The Experience of Children in a Joint-Custody Arrangement: A Report of a Study," *American Journal of Orthopsychiatry*, vol. 5, no. 3 (July, 1981), pp. 403–415, is a report of a pilot study; she is now in the midst of a much larger study of the adjustment of children to the binuclear family.

I have cited several times the work of Joseph Goldstein, Anna Freud, and Albert J. Solnit, *Beyond the Best Interests of the Child* (New York: Free Press, 1979), a brilliantly organized—but in my view misguided—attack on the disjoined family. They have identified the problem, but I think their solution is worse than the problem itself.

Another kind of book is written by family therapists and others who run workshops for the families of divorce. They tend to be how-to books. For example, Edith Atkin and Estelle Rubin wrote *Part-Time Father* (New York: Vanguard Press, 1976); psychotherapist Persia Woolley wrote *The Custody Handbook* (New York: Summit Books, 1979); and psychotherapist Isolina Ricci produced *Mom's House, Dad's House, Making Shared Custody Work* (New York: Macmillan, 1980), which is a plea for the binuclear family.

Another side to the plea for the binuclear family is a

moving book by Mel Roman and William Haddad, *The Disposable Parent: the Case for Joint Custody* (New York: Holt, Rinehart and Winston, 1978). Ciji Ware (*Sharing Parenthood After Divorce* [New York: Viking, 1982]), herself an active co-parent, has scouted out and put together what seems like all the information now available on the subject of joint custody. It is required reading for anyone involved in a binuclear family.

The literature on the stepfamily remains scanty. One early good book was William C. Smith's *The Stepchild* (Chicago: University of Chicago Press, 1953). It looks into the stepchild in folklore and literature as well as into the stepchild's adjustment. In 1964, Anne W. Simon provided *Stepchild in the Family* (New York: Odyssey Press).

The literature on the stepfamily entered a new phase when Emily B. Visher and John S. Visher published *Stepfamilies: A Guide to Working with Stepparents and Stepchildren* (New York: Brunner/Mazel, 1979). The Vishers, themselves stepparents to one another's children, are particularly well qualified to write on this topic. He is a psychiatrist, she a clinical psychologist. Both specialize in stepfamilies, and together they run highly successful workshops, some primarily for therapists, others for the stepfamily members themselves. They founded the Stepfamily Association of America. They were my primary mentors on the subject of the stepfamily and this book owes much to their guidance.

Elizabeth Einstein's *The Stepfamily: Living, Loving and Learning* (New York: Macmillan, 1982) is a good modern summary. Other important information about the stepfamily can be found in Clifford Sager's *Marriage Contracts and Couple Relationships* (New York: Brunner/Mazel, 1976); his "Remarriage Revisited," *Family and Child Mental Health Journal*, vol. 6 (1980), pp. 19–33, is also useful. Phyllis N. Stern's doctoral dissertation in nursing at the Medical School, University of California, San Francisco, is extremely useful for its information about discipline in stepfamily households. Two pieces of it are generally available: an abstract called "Integrative Discipline in Stepfathers and Fathers" (*Dissertation Abstracts International*, 1977-B: 4491-B, #77-5, 276) and an article, "Stepfather Families: Integration around Child Discipline," *Issues in Mental Health Nursing*, vol. 1, no. 2 (1980), pp. 49–56. A first-rate how-to book is *Living in Step* by Ruth Roosevelt and Jeannette Lofas (New York: McGraw-Hill, 1981); that book contains both useful analysis and good advice. A study of stepfathers in San Diego in the middle seventies (of which I was the stepfather) turned up some interesting information that is well summarized in Herbert Yahraes, "Stepfathers as Parents," *Families Today*, DHEW publication no. ADM 79-897, 1979. The Stepfamily Association of America maintains a partly annotated bibliography that is available from the Association, c/o Mala Burt, 28 Allegheny Ave., Suite 1307, Baltimore, MD 21204.

The family is the most central of all human social institutions. One of the tasks of both behavioral scientists and journalists in the next years is to continue the process of separating what we know about it from social myths and psychological fears.

Index